A DOOR

by Aaron Shurin

Woman on Fire
The Night Sun
Toot Suite
Giving Up the Ghost
The Graces
Codex
Elsewhere
A's Dream
Narrativity
Into Distances
Unbound: a Book of AIDS
Involuntary Lyrics
The Paradise of Forms
A Door

AARON SHURIN

A DOOR

Talisman House, Publishers
Jersey City, New Jersey

Published in the United States of America by
                    Talisman House, Publishers
                    P.O. Box 3157
                    Jersey City, New Jersey 07303-3157

Manufactured in the United Sates of America
Printed on acid-free paper

Library of Congress Cataloging-in-Publication Data

Shurin, Aaron, 1947-
    A door / Aaron Shurin
        p. cm.
    ISBN 1-58498-009-5 (acid-free paper) — ISBN 1-58498-008-7 (pbk. : acid-
free paper)
        I. Title

PS3569.H86 D66 2000
811'.54—dc21

                                                    00-044304

ACKNOWLEDGMENTS

The author expresses his appreciation to the following journals in which some of this work originally appeared:

Apex of the M, Arshile, Central Park, Columbia Poetry Review, Conjunctions, Coracle, disturbed guillotine, Five Fingers Review, Grand Street, Hambone, Ink, Long News: in the Short Century, Magazine, Mirage, New American Writing, Notus, SFSU Review, Sakura: Japanese Poetry Review, Some Weird Sin, Sulfur, Talisman, Talus, Tape, To, The World, Tyuonyi, and *Zyzzyva*

as well as the anthologies *From the Other Side of the Century, The Art of Practice, Subliminal Time: o 4,* and *The Gertrude Stein Awards in Innovative American Writing*

and the collection *The Paradise of Forms: Selected Poems* (Talisman House, 1999).

The author also gratefully acknowledges the Wallace Alexander Gerbode Foundation for its support through the Gerbode Poetry Prize.

CONTENTS

Threshold . . . 1

Opened . . . 3

Prelude . . . 4

The Self . . . 5

There Among . . . 9

Ninth Life . . . 10

Absolute Monarch . . . 14

As She . . . 15

Nocturne . . . 16

Spring Nude . . . 17

Riders . . . 19

Fin de Siècle . . . 21

Her Own . . . 23

Overlooking the Sea Next to Mine . . . 30

An Adolescence . . . 32

A Door . . . 34

The Last Head I Painted . . . 46

Soliloquy . . . 47

The Night Mixing . . . 48

The Bride of Frank . . . 49

Medium Green . . . 51

Chances (I) . . . 53

Chances (II) . . . 55

Chances (III) . . . 56

Smoke Signals . . . 57

Slim Ceremony . . . 58

Tell Me . . . 60

"In a Little Stream of Ascending Air" . . . 61

Pele's Smile . . . 62

To John . . . 63

To John . . . 64

To John . . . 65

To John . . . 66

To John . . . 67

Man of the House . . . 68

Legend . . . 69

Red Geraniums . . . 70

Impromptu . . . 71

Little Madrigal . . . 72

Fade . . . 73

No Place Like Noon . . . 74

Subliminal Sweat . . . 75

High Heels . . . 78

One More Step . . . 81

Human Immune . . . 82

American Things . . . 88

Jinnee . . . 89

The Wanderer's Necklace . . . 91

A DOOR

"called up of the float of the brain of the world"

—Walt Whitman

THRESHOLD

I listen every ten seconds to the dahlias — birds in a nest — and little by little recognize the road in the distance, smaller, scattered into words, competent. On the table a cloudy glass is distinguished from its ring on the napkin by regular intervals coiled in place.

Militant home life — localized pleasures — can't be interpreted through the window. Significance is on the pink wall with irregular pulsations of light. A little cloud of dust stops for a moment outside the door straining at its hinges.

Your comrade — my struggling body — is banging against the skin of a drum. Those songs flush the milky blueness out of insomnia. The skin of the wing vanishes through sleep or consummation.

You wrote, and the loops of that stream impatient to roam the world were pushing some detail into place: she rubs herself with coconut oil. She stood on tiptoe, covered with sun. She laughed sprawling in cotton shorts full of moist sand.

His head resting on his folded arms — easy familiarity — warm path — shower of petals — as the round shadow dropping from a lamp will soon dissolve in light — hesitated and spoke, absolving the upturned trees.

His roving eyes streamed down the shore, adding maturity as I wiped my neck in the presence of detachment. When we dive we keep our unexpected eyes open. A stroke of work. A fragment of homage capable of moonlight.

Will you be warm enough? In the shape of a body a drama of gestation communicated themselves to me. The eucalyptus air —

electric moths — is striking a passing car. Her bare arm and the incomparable scarf drive on through that corolla.

The rising landscape — gesture of rain — watched them trickling down. Then rubbed with that sea my house smokes, taking the wind away from the present without looking back. You remain on the threshold between us to fill my cupped hands.

OPENED

Back and forth to look out — desire nothing — to the place opened leaving white gaps into the cool of the evening breeze. The most moral deed was standing in two worlds.

He was a changing man and he grasped the window frame. Heads could see boys on the roofs no longer interested in him — forgotten events — so that the stores were closed, announcing mobilization, men walking. They stood outside — merchandise — across a single person in battle dress, covered with a cold light about stomach sweat.

She spoke with the voice of a man, pushed her way in. She stood on the table but signified assistance — being available — hung a picture of sunlight around his neck, swept the floor, read the trembling paper in his hands. This man — he raised the book — reading a book was frightened — attracted her — of the great cities — in an attic room until eleven o'clock on the square. She began to spread on the chair an account of America.

Her fingers like rich brides touch the walls. On the bed in his room — her own room — he was being extended — neither beginning nor end — slanting high in the window their shining attributes — it was summer — a breeze was blowing.

PRELUDE

O I mean devoted to the front — with erasures — accurate plunge and compel eyes under its surface — who ringing for him a gesticulated sunset or swing of flanks and *that* music — O I mean examining their contents from my morning porch bent head, signing an agreement with tremulous commentary — when the weave intercoils in the world a person upstairs and energy in the living room. I mean the open door from the slippery threshold presented morning, a red car.

Lowering my pencil — I was already finished — the usual questions were fired at me. Instead I asked a moody boy — stunning viscera — "Do you have a mental picture of pulling off winter clothes finger by finger?" I wanted chocolate cookies, a brandy, a minute of a marital scene, view from a window.

Sitting with a book and its shadows moving up and down in lamplight — swinging arms of his friendship — O I mean one night I began squirting at other people from my swivel chair. I salute in the middle of a grocery store raw carrots. His dignity of heart constituted a mask in keeping with the harmonies of manliness fashion — neck, I mean, profile mountain, leonine — by the same forces of perfection which color his verse. I'm wearing white slacks and sunglasses, preserved from the skulls around me. I'm witnessing a fusion across the table — enthroned in adjacent positions — his fluid fingers, I mean, which could dissolve by tossing it in the air . . .

THE SELF

I.

In the year appointed a man on the road to perfection was neglected. He permitted indifference in order to make the reader understand youth. The little boys were slaves to hard-faced men. In action, language was the most heinous crime.

This boy with dark curling hair, slender air, physical will, wild enthusiasm, was reading poetry in the streaming wind — river glide past him running melancholy — pressing his hands together liked to call himself "emancipation-of-the-people". He had tears. He had disgust. He had agreeable terror.

Other monsters like you and me rendered these inventions fascinating — flame of the air called up by a young voice — swaying waist while eyes drank — their arms interlocked through the topmost leaves beneath his touch, to study the names of things and examine his rumpled clothes. His gestures were moral expressions who wanted to tidy up every table and chair. He followed them until they sank, worn out by his expenditure of energy.

I'm an outcast, but my mother believes me. Beauty upholds the ceremonies it adorns. I enter into an intimacy — being his imagination — filled with good intentions and faults of prosody — twined around a neighboring pine — to the physical tones and carry them out of bounds. I desire an envelope sealed with the sentence of expulsion.

When he sat down he wrote "young man". The young man with dramatic gestures was put on the table. What are they? I copied them out of a book this morning. I loved a being. He was astounded. It was all he had to live on.

It's not love that differentiates him but scenery. One would need to be nineteen years old. The following nights were clear and bright. He went for a walk in that city.

II.

Too dazzling for the emotions which surround him, human operations began an intolerable itch — rebellious conscience — my humility is complete as I change the lives of others. His delight mapped out the improvement of the country to conquer every heart — in place of a lance he carried martyrdom — stuffed with pamphlets, and into the hood of an old cloak the smile of pity freed him from remorse.

He stood before the exile's bags and boxes. A heap of laws adopted the paternal tone. In the eyes of a young man I myself am dust — wildness of the mountain pools was personal property — from the windows the sea advanced the most violent epithets. The bony stranger set off on long expeditions, each containing a remedy, and a mast and sail above.

Having loaded them into the summer sky he swayed seaward. Spheres — surfaces — tenuous — float until they broke and vanished. The greens and golds of autumn winds became unbearable.

I'll go with you, enchanted like a boy. I have endless theories to introduce to stories.

III.

In certain countries children are the devil; in his own heart he forgot both time and place. It was too late to go to your circle of beauties.

Sometimes the poem opened the little pocket on the love text which sweetens the night — these walks these talks — of the luxury against an environment — which he imagined as scattered throughout the universe, exquisite and perfect and a disappointment.

A great slab of hazel eyes cultivated precision.

Of silence there comes a moment when a picture of spiritual order may write what I please. He wove around these webs bonds of rage. Four in the afternoon slowly faded away.

Roads, armies, fields, gowns, slept in his place. The big stove in darkness beat against the windows. I hope to live many years in health, virtuous, depraved.

He talked of frightening each other: somebody had been pulled down the stairs by an invisible hand. He talked of terror of communication with the outcasts: a letter was waiting on the pavement looking for him.

This blessing, this reward, this purpose, these monies, his expectations, the relations, the thousands of pounds, this judgment, astonishment, forgiveness, this bitter form, this child, this danger, this atmosphere, this frame.

I am worthy of your love.

THERE AMONG

She had to — this round object — beginning again — write.

A being unscrewing the makers with one heavy arm full of papers in the sunshine under the hollyhocks she remembered. Power was in her imaginary baton striking the blotted hour — speed of the morning — collecting evidence, crossing whole families, crawling beneath vagrants stretched on her elbows, hunted, frozen, and parts the tall blades.

But to go these fragmentary judgments somebody else continuously their existence brought together she did it, but to whom? She had become sheathed, tinted, was ajar, and stood still. A chest of drawers could still see her, and offices, and her point-of-view books, and her mother.

These people made her say it. For the light in the commodities twitched, having their underworld substance and being window panes — let him pass — accumulated treasures shifting, and it made her running water push forward — she was a rider — as if people were marching yet had been dying. She was watching, pouring the window open, immediately possible.

And on the submerged city going without and with expectations ceremony spread. A glass of water shook. One gull — silence — swooped a white tunnel. They are signaling to be opened. She was there.

NINTH LIFE

Everyone went by holding a white bag, aware of the garbage on the street. The wind in the mesh with low voices bearing absurd blossoms surrounded their heads. To gain a sense of proportion — organized beauty — she visualized herself visible as she stood on the corner — an airplane dangled above — spike-haired by the force of this pain — her eyes raised, spread-eagled with concentration. She was forming a grid to separate the pictures of dinner and his stomach. There was no shelter to protect you from the sight of customers. Their personalities flashed and clotted with each step. The blue power unfolded into her bone — she bit her nails — and opened both hands. Doors snapped up like wings. She walked back to the apartment.

Each sought one of the bodies and fastened itself in the direction of the heads. They arose they are handsome his expressionless voice protruding muscles. He lays the eggs himself. Into this aperture I feel what he would feel. She felt provocative, tossing it to the floor. His nose was transpiring between them — I'm itchy — her legs of satisfaction finding honey within the spirit. From the first instant she felt brilliant, juicing forward on all fours, positioned herself for perpetual excitement toward his sniff. She was beginning to feel like a young girl with both hands. Her whole body was flinging her fingers. When your body becomes useless you are a mass of stupid flesh. The moons the stars were created for this purpose. She lay in her way to the outer world, relaxed on its back.

I gaze on the horizon whenever I light up a cigarette. I was fabulous with praise who saturated my ego, driven by an insatiable libido. Wails of queens echoed through royal tombs. A woman began to talk like an eternity — in a leather miniskirt lit up with hope — I was making my debut every evening — the most glorious holiday — to the sound of long strands of summer rain as I rubbed the sleep from my eyes. Then she crossed to the windows that I called home, lush from a cluster of firework rose bushes between two palms, and if I wasn't the fallen fruits I swung on the vines. When mobs of strange-looking people melted together I was just a little thing and fall to the ground. Separated by curtains I found it very theatrical.

"What are your parents like?" "I don't know. My father has a prick." She began a history characterized by abandoned everywhere. He rolled over on his masochist stomach, dismantling the couch. Her body stupid something mutual pleasure was hostility. She opened the window — why is this happening — that you don't talk together — her opened mouth released her beside the malodorous roses. In reality, beside him in the car, he turned on the radio. Impossible conversations made gestures up the wall. A little girl cocoon invented characters. Her bloomed scenes spiraled and froze. She was making mayonnaise at the knees. The air was sprouting a designer sheet and an aluminum chair. He turned on the radio. She stroked his shoulder.

Unloosed from their lashing the body arrested his fall. With the strength of desperation his hand holds a leather belt snapping at its outer end — equipment of muscles high courage — where he lay upon his unnatural belly, attracted to a small cluster of familiar lines. In the shelter of the clump of the girl he knew nothing. The thing he had witnessed strode toward a door. Two figures leading to the chamber through the head. She raised her eyes — the singing girl — she was unable to breathe but kept laughing — spilling up from the bed and began walking toward the door. I think I'll go out. I can hardly talk. She carried two glasses into the living room. Beautiful skin drop down toward the rug. They gobbled that expression on her face.

That day — seeing the men that way — harbored inside me with a maniacal glaze — one of our rehearsals — came into my room shortly after I woke, his adamant eyes leaned into me. The floorboard jaw muscles creaked. Full of defiance like a scratch I spilled drama — an individual is condemned — no matter how many times I closed my eyes he was doing back flips out the grimy bus window. I had no ambition as we pulled black air out of the rain. She moaned herself from the chair. Her tongue licked the hairs. Sinewy legs were just the beginning. Buzzards watched our once graceful homes. Pinned between hulks, pleading into the phone, the buildings grew larger but the streets empathized with a park bench. Bodies make ends meet. I decided to stand on the street.

Her body with the uptilted chin gushed, squeezed her innermost life into her face with lipstick. Her head threw back — outside of this place — balanced on one spike to screw around her checked dress. "I do something," she said, clutching a red purse. The swinging shapes through the slats were personal effects, as one bird with its hooked beak tried to picture her in her apartment. Swirling across her back, her mouth arranged in laughter. People were eating and yelling on the opposite side of the street. They had some things to do, surprised at the animal smell. Her body, respectful — she'd gone there — suffered from nostalgia. The late afternoon was flapping open close to a fashionable cafe. A tall girl immediately raced to a corner table.

"The gods sent me," he replied, "but I failed to recognize you." She had heard the voice in command behind a turn in the stairway. She looked down from above upon the finest points of his naked body. Moonlight flooded their feeding troughs. She had the power to quicken poor lumps dominated by the brain. The girl was rising above the top of the wall — stream weight human endeavor short of perfection — caught by a current of air drifting toward headless things. He should be a god but that other world was ready to question his preeminence. She touched his arm hoping for that reward. The high white walls were sentinels of other buildings. "I don't know what city this is," and leaned with her chin resting across the balcony, "but I was expecting it."

In the world and the thought of its head I'd completely forgotten what had happened, the city seemed so quiet. No one understood what they'd just seen, with its mouth open. Waving her arms into the air with powdered cheeks on the corner talking to what was happening in the immediate environment — flickering intersection — she unlodged the mess with the back of her hand, and kept walking. A stump could wear one of those blue uniforms. The pavement applied to any position except my translucent skin. Aspiration while strolling was becoming impossible, over my eye where the lid falls. One day with its legs in the air I was more like a real person. A revolving door was wearing my lipstick. I was not coming back.

ABSOLUTE MONARCH

The thoughts he told himself put him in spirits. He began to understand flowering plants which possess the ceiling in perfect solitude, a pink and grey attention unconscious of his existence. "Do you lay your commands on me?" and ran his fingers through his hair. He wanted the order of forebodings breathed graciously that cling to the hem of your dress; or a mixture of humility and sins to initiate him into the mysteries of absolution. A back staircase infatuated with accomplices — one charming hand pulsed, bare mechanism.

The dinner table set up taking the field. Holes in the curtain can have a little talk:

"The savannahs of dinner cultivate the vineyards."

"Stammering some words he wavered and doubted; failed to catch their meaning."

"Three times bread took him by surprise: nothing was happening as a piece, so minds are powerless."

Join love thereto.

As for keeping the secret: they were all about you; the reddest bird-nesting drawers and boxes, cracking and sucking pleasure. That slow glittering hoard, just as it happened . . .

Felt in his pockets, flung down on the table a pebble, exactly where the brain places it.

AS SHE

The place stream there as she slid into the window seat. Grazed backwards. Out of her eyes faith and so on — broke into a smile the whole weekend she had an appetite for.

Under her face in that position extending along the front from long practice approving her transformation at the way her shoulders had straightened for my arrival that night, a season suggested a polka dot scarf. Someone comes — a different school, different teachers — being swiftly the kid that never was — with an air of charming brightness about nothing, the way they spoke, gestured — then jump on his back — skimming against the furniture, publicly and officially twirling a baton. She began to unravel — up her rosy masochism, shudder expunging blushing — searching and feeling in the same place her shivery appeal.

The surrounding area was lying out in the open; she leaned her head out of the window, air . . .

NOCTURNE

Being far away in bed you've been through my ideal — this morning I dream about a waltz — to walk over my body with your polished voice ascending. It isn't a matter of grief but near you I'm lazy. Your most warmth mouth, in the head of which echoes could ruin my reputation.

Death is the opposite of complaining, little face, but one must have resemblance. The greatest luxury is noise (a bird's gliding by a balcony) on a road off the track in falsetto. Little bells around the neck collect orbits. The waves here are enormous and uniform; I kiss you on both impressions.

All the trees in the sky are dressed for summer. Everything else is trailing vines — I'll have the sea. Here I am, pale as always, shaped like a small window. Repair to my pearly bed, tell him to measure out whole days and evenings.

From the beginning the skies or the fact of the skies went everyday to pose for good sense or good health. Creatures play airs in serious thing. Moderation is necessary but your stairway rises offering trills — decorations stopping to chat — and my bedroom is at everyone's disposition — drowned and tuned to fog or fresh air. I'd like to have met you somewhere, dropping from drowsiness.

Friendship's endless corridors of old portraits — strings and pegs — are being changed to libraries, chairs, dinners, my apartment, a passport. I give you anything you want — my body opened — the little waltz marked with your shoulders — unleashed and modulated to repose . . .

SPRING NUDE

Violent highlights: the singer's blue hips. Deep grid of her sweater — a heart pulses up — in the early stages through fog through his future career through symbolic projection, moving free of shapes. The visible would remain lodged inside him. Hers are bathed in the receding dark.

He'd survived as an edge between competing colors. A hybrid of adolescent rejection, nude. I looked hard at my own hand finding abstractions — generated by the poetry — it was a social thing — horizontally isolated but banded with lines, the messy life of objects until he found a representational spot: rooftops.

He was disappointed about the marvelous heads out of doors, then moved forward. A woman became a view declared complete. Men turn their eyes to the high window. I could open a door of dialogue again.

I remember I hit the irrational ceiling — wasn't going to cooperate — indeterminate interior to one side of a bifurcated gender. A figure dragged to the surface — all familiar form — egg-faced in her pantaloons — red squirts, buttery atmosphere — she saws her instrument, oblivious with concentration. The background becomes tighter, nervous with hindsight, enlarged.

She was a remnant in uninflected space, low on the horizon — its trajectory into the ground released her. I arrived leaner in the shifting heat, splattered with similarities, converted into hair and face.

Pool within boundaries.

The day after he was crowded with awkward poses. On the roof of a nearby building the bright sun.

RIDERS

I wore them because the smell of saliva on them had parallel with their bodies. Once you were in those wings you knew all you needed to know about preadolescent blue pajamas. I lay in bed sleeping and waking, salt and pepper. Hairs made me feel grown up.

When anyone spoke of my cousins I was watching a figure emerge sideways — long expanse of his back tearing up the kitchen — expelled prickly sweat as my knee against — pulled the cinch tight till it flew like streamers behind me.

He'd written the text on his body I pulled a book from the shelf into my private mythology. I'm in a downtown hotel. He comes to visit us. I was scolded. Glances of the old men. I was undressed beside the public pool. The restrooms holiday three sons friendships quick hug narrow hips stay over living room couch enormous poppies confidante clutching my hand between the doorway and the bed.

All identification had been long forbidden and secured. I sat in a chair in the accounting of simultaneous feeling. Diverted from refusal as inevitably as ill-prepared, by some quirk of natural ability through dark brown eyes. He is my music, a box of pastels, draped kimono, red vase, linen sheets, falcon fate, epitaph, sailor, short pants, fish smell, rhyme word, Italian sonnet, spin cycle, black grease, ball point, back stairway, towered wall, hotel room, my bookcase I'm lying on the couch my field of daffodils I put my empty lips against his until my eyes are swollen shut, his shoulders pinned me, smell of neck hair and dog smell — tell me how to breathe — one of their own — tight around our legs — older than we were . . .

". . . their tangled manes by force of wind
        aslant from their extended necks . . ."

FIN DE SIÈCLE

It's as though the wandering sky I knew whose gliding companions mimic the clouds seemed to be watching its reflections in the window — I'll dream of kisses — making my thoughts hang and ripen into cities. O you underworld arsenals, days split their flowering skin of tremendous fields — the grandeur of my poses pure mirrors — towards the rival sun. I'm imperfect in my floating perfumes and delirium. I love memory.

Who whose smooth invitation fattened up by fertility goes spreading under the polished sky classical lessons — it was summer — and made the tolling blaze at the end of the corridor drink space — the body was alive and multiplying — penetrating image of the year a sun lies on anything that's green. I was lamenting winter.

When I breathe my nostrils people the dark world that's absent with human reposes. There came a frame — it be the work — in which myself with frowning eyebrows give you appearance — then you lay under my destiny as a river sheds hot water. I love a man choked like a forge. I believe you open the door from fear alone.

In those times that sun lodged in him are one flaming hillside — pouring essence on the floor — and the shivering falsetto paintings flourish in his simple studio. Afterwards, the metaphysical skies will be heavy with farewells.

It is, despite his meditating efforts, slanting winter. Girl of swishing tatters and men are making the clouds tinkle. Banging himself and stumbling under the suspended sky he was not a temple but high in their midst. I, whose memory was once entrancing, was standing in allegory and smeared with my own image. The wincing sky, all its entrances exits. In the enemy sky, soup of streetlamps and bedrooms.

21

They say I'm submerged through those mirrors, windows, and draperies. None of these things can equal the tender sky. You make me think of sweeping boas, thud of summer light, slumber jars. Pillow sabbath. Opium labyrinth. Foaming bread or wine.

Oh and on things the morning in parallel-beam glides towards the sun and hardens. It was in the past, double, of an afternoon bliss — one of those recitals — and which you feel yourself coming to shaped like a crown.

Someone appears; the slower atmosphere of significant gravity.
You are my equal. Take me away, filled with appetite and infancy.

HER OWN

I.

She was rescued, reaching out like burning straw. And each challenge from the bondages of form — a garden scene — has a pink unspoiled face that would have been burned.

Frances — her head is mysteriously masculine — wanted drastic statements. She would initiate each love with the same man: weary consent of her first kiss. She took on fifty pounds and dramatized herself. Bare feet were cut straight from the shoulder — I'm afraid of your bed like a drug — her own path had sexually ambivalent separate rooms.

She isn't crying to follow the musical phrase. It was a situation where witches when they met around the room recognized what she had expected — open the door and brush your shoulder — instinctively festive who were going to have behavior or scandal. Frances liked her costume. She's abstracted down the museum steps, tossing away her name.

It's the pace, the shift; it's of the ways. The sands are clear, the winds would dominate their evenings.

In a hotel her world was actual experiences in the corridors — she loses a watch and swallows figs — unrelinquished objects — but if hands touched me his shaggy omnipotence was forced to accept a secondary role. The delayed arrival of private feelings had infringed upon his domain. I've seen this sniffing thing move to spasms.

I would say — both as a person and a mind — when one reads in sublime ways the universal rights were like commands. Frances washes in on the power struggles of a soft summer night. I shall cut you dead if each had a separate identity.

One summer evening she felt the cold union of my thoughts against the formless rocks. They were the women in his descriptions of clothes, eating men. The point of departure was hanging over them, given the massacres. She wanted to become a great lover as a person in a real world.

You were
to me
burned silence
perfect craft, waving her arms
who and speech had to
out her ancient eyes
as a woman, I mean,
cerebral
inside the circle of her perpetual separation.

There are more dimensions — and that did it — she'd been given the opportunity. Within the tangles immediate friendship of two lives.

II.

She recognized the door opened; first words were the clairvoyant
young woman twisted in coils commanding hard red lips: *merge into
your little forest.* Yesterday, it meant so much to be stretched before
her.

In the house of the intellect the mind next door was vacant. Frances
— chafed, blown, discovering the magnetic line — crouching by the
hurt leaves — she may have felt guilty — becomes a daemon — one
side of her — then this other thing comes. My dear bombshell, who
is she, this ghost of an idea? I'm starving for her shaken nerves —
her flowers — I could be healed upon her traces.

In an enormous house prodigious women sit, deployed all over. She
was forced to undergo satins on an extravagant narrow bed. It fell
carefully seeking honey. She admired anonymous women on a
survival basis.

It was beneath her riches
penetrated vistas, herself a child
hushed, it was a fissure
raising flowers she wanted
her entrance, their patterns.

Her work — her hand — tore into pieces a single egg, and sunlight
in the little room let go. When I tried to explain it was as though
through water dismissed where she floated — Frances disembod-
ied, protected, receiving, together with her broken past to break-in
a brain. Accuse her of having a brain. There was an air she called
power that hung like grapes. It's more than that person, so slender
and solid — length of legs in their pride in the liquid arch — she
contemplated the physical act to my wondering eyes, impersonally,
her skirts held high.

III.

On the verge of her head she had taken up — you might say psychi-
cally — my bed. This girl — but it was I — was she really disassoci-
ated from my inner vision — stuck in my eye — cut her long hair,
passed. Then, rather grand in her speech: *I set you free.*

She had a boyhood, searching for "self-reliant", "rough", "hand-
some". Her new expanding life came to California. She can remem-
ber the sea — appalled emptiness — on a cliff, plunge her into
observations — in themselves romantic shapes, stamped with
history — shrinking from a masculine or a feminine gesture? She
smiled. It's the thing itself accomplishing the tasks we achieve.

It's there whom nothing would change, not of love, but ideas. She
wanted to believe that everything is possible. *She* be a marriage.

In the world, where men would be the most outspoken, she clashed
by night, throwing herself around, her sympathy displaying her
charms in other directions. Warmer, her equal rock structures —
I'm a respectable outcast — Frances, a figure of concealment,
chooses to reveal obscure passion. She considered living together as
man and wife.

Frances knows more about it than I do. The person she happens to
be becomes another person. Entire physical histories want them to
be happy.

Lovers aren't whimsical
for your sweetness
of respect
has lost itself in a strange field
yes, I shout my ways
since a dress, a bird, a hat, accompanying
the stance, made her feel

actuality of any kind.
Evening wrap. Bright night air.

We — perverse fate given us — returned to write her story as if she owned the city. Frances, ask me again, it would be good to see someone from home.

Her touch melts toward the shadow rocks.

She's a hive of them. With its flickering kiss, created for her, on the edge of personal patterns.

IV.

Her face — just you — against hair, reminds herself of an internal battle: fire (other people) and air (poetic mind).

A laboratory — Frances has a room above — across the rooftops by moonlight she became increasingly attractive. I think the writhing gods had a mother fixation. I have infinite faith in our harassed lives, separated from your silver curtain. *Be* your armies — she calls "my world" — cinematic lights — on the sidewalk under the humane lights she was a psychic kingdom, and projects her swan going on. She shook all over, at the coffee shop and in her journal.

She was sitting at a table she said there is nothing now but to fight. Her short cropped head was oracular. That shabby woman in royal robes of her girlhood.

There was music. There was this desk. The world was a place where Frances — the unbelievable — existed.

There was another world. She dispersed doors — move two ways — I would never have found — she came ahead to find a place for you.

I saw some other places. Her great eyelids as though it were solid flesh. Her gaunt beauty would stare on the street, no lapses. Was that her woman? The lover was a likeness, her abbreviations.

She felt strong enough to strike out on her own.

V.

In the darkened streets she would be a companion of wet weather
and literature — the gift of place — she had a complement in the
hills, a reason for her travels. Sunsets, mountains, permitted her
aesthetic reactions; according to her own pattern Frances blows
oranges from blue skies.

Along the glass passageway she wanted to get down to work. I have
a window, a beamed ceiling, an opposite shore. They seem to have
me in a private house within which she views her daily life. Her
observations spread wings, identified with the story, likes people,
will make anything, is created in the doorway. I'm younger than
before we started our walk.

Here's a journal called The Gossiping Paths. It was her youth. She
laid the book aside. It could put itself down, having seen her for
forty years.

She answered:
Something in this century
didn't take place.
They're nice people
for the day.
Little attentions
don't squeal.
I am enthusiastic.

Through tremor and vibration — last ardor — the person reflected
her drama. Frances in the night, examine yourself closely. The
unspecified work flows. I'm so glad I saw her inevitable hands.

OVERLOOKING THE SEA NEXT TO MINE

I'm sitting down I'm doing it I find her face equals the face in the presence of a person. The man in one's heart is adjectives. My stomach is sacrificed again to my mouth on waking.

I say to myself: there's a little woman on crescendo, propelled by my fear. Penetrating the body has its reasons unknown to the body. What issues from my mouth expresses him again — kissing your eyes, sitting on your lap, was the beginning of the French language.

Lives bloom to release pleasures; for the sake of elegance it hurts my feelings. The universe of the hours have built your physical presence. My book of distinctive words by themselves — all the feelings I hide from you — is drooping with tenderness, but the next kiss is fresh.

Someone gets filled with heraldic devices:
— one hand in a bathtub
— sunlight closely on that earthworm
— took the train and walked in on a room at the back of the house
— between two women examining your gift of sympathy
The volume of his thigh is beginning to produce music: when it reaches us I might kiss your psychological hands.

Picking up crumpled newspapers — over the dialogue between the locomotive and the woman in the square — from the whirling cocoon of necromantic language — (accept us and charm us) — each inland sea has sent you a flock of pigeons, shaken by grief, glimpsing a face, finding resemblances . . .

It's an impossible task, silence, and would the detour be natural? Her theatrical soul and melody were both invited to dinner. I may spend September in the memories.

AN ADOLESCENCE

The doorway — the truth — was domestic but his son was a chain of events. He would point to the certificate of belonging signed by himself — scattered tribesmen — of a sunlight augury in a timid smile — nestles protectively around his brother's neck — his exorbitant mother completely known and real.

That island of a normal life on a sheet of black paper in flames. In my unctuous room scent of the cherries stained glass with the overtall summer evening — beyond the control of international law — where the narrative of an actual memory had a temperature and cool skin, on which the recovery of my father's kiss, for having been denied, is open. The involuntary family was asking for pity in a causal relation to art.

From the grocery to the only bookshop shadows of an ancient clock; a portion of the wall is the nineteenth century and the purplish floor is blown to pieces. In the intermittent hot rain appear roofbeams, a glowing window where the river was his garden — lock himself in — heroic pleasures — in the underground chamber of the boys and girls and brother — on the opposite side, reflected, pink, fusing . . .

He, by some predisposition who must be imprisoned and made powerless, is the only feeling which can never be returned, rejected a part of himself, an inventory of the contents translated for him by all of the people I love, who have no feelings for the pleasures of affection but are faithful to the memories.

And at his bedside at night the idol of his confession album is striving for indulgence. Forbidden lilacs where the materials for real comparison are scanty. One was running, another chasing, but his words were composed of boys. Double muscles, polite conversation and the rumbling barbarian verbal contours — booing and applause — skirts sweeping the gravel of his wasted time. I was in bed trying to pull him back, satisfied with vague sensations.

Everything is transformed below his window by the stains of these sleeping things. He was no longer a schoolboy but a young man with blue eyes. The phenomenal world is the equivalent of my phrases. I was my temporary self.

A DOOR

Once — I move back in time — caught within a circle — I can be like some traveler after the vestiges — ageing planet — the street wasn't just a thoroughfare, it was a place where people lived. A journey occurs in the social hierarchy between house and bush. Each mound glistening through the grass, set among loose stones, almost vertical cliffs . . .

Her gown pinches her waist to represent a crescent moon. Eyelids between her breasts, dropping down the mountains. She inspects nets made of hairs — crackles under the sound of sparks — walls inlaid with glass winds, we'd stare at the sun . . .

Someone didn't follow him into the kitchen, though I adored vigorous beauty. That it looked as if it would crack with scintillated youth — us their object — he watched, generated in the darkness by one hand, to our swarming garments part of us a third person — we let them fall — what's called triumph — making both our shame and our glory for a long time in a room. Smiling with sweat, of whose virtue we partook . . .

She starts towards the bedroom, but doesn't move — breeze comes up with two drinks, looking for Johnny. Here you are beautiful, as he starts past the twin beds. He holds onto him, throws her arms around his neck through the door . . .

I wonder how at one time we're our own lives and a shadow, the steep hillside to a saucerlike plain to a fortified river. The blood smell upon your face is honey to stinging bees. Sitting on a stool in the red light of sunset he pointed to another stool. He's eaten his tongue, he must listen to rumors playing on the word . . .

And we got to talking, plucking at his tweed sleeve — grossed seven grand with that puzzled grin — took the elevator upstairs and sat down again. I put my head down against sandwiches and apple pie. It wasn't like anything, it wasn't like real poetry . . .

The house filled with poppyseed rolls I baked myself, scraps of meat, hiccups or headaches. Two kids have long tongues and go home in the evening. I took my bread — the moon started to pound through the cracks — each tiny bone came nearer — as though I'd dropped from the roof — on her white lips a smile. You might accumulate a bucket . . .

And the veiling wind draws water into the clouds. It was ocean above the waters. They sprinkled their foreheads, with your mother's bones behind you. They covered their heads — their hardness — out of the quiver of this memory my boy came down causing love all the way — through the hiding places — who's your curious charm . . .

We've had chestnut trees and candles — in splinters on a mirror — and will hurl itself at the period blossoms to evoke the scorching in progress. The wrinkled cherries swoon away, a sky in possession behind the inflated foreground. The creamy emptiness resembling a road, a conversation, a dozen homonyms, a nightbird cries in broad daylight, abandoning moderation . . .

We had only to stretch our hands to establish contact with the landscape. It's the tenderest hue of uncertain fragility — brown and pink against the ravages of emerald and white. I tramped over the ground — conveyed to me by its fragrance, not its shapes — in which the most telling posture was the opposite direction, uneven, a series of sharp tiers clinging to the coastal wall. He closes it with one key, its paradisal state providing fuel for crucibles . . .

A seductive man confesses to understanding nothing about plea-sure. I'm not a woman but a world. Your chastity would walk into an olive grove, demanding sacrifice — bend down to receive a certain vertigo — at which your hand fill my thirst aimed at moving his tender wounds. One received an order, was converted through an apparition, head still bowed . . .

I call it a generative organ — the luminosity of which would have hatched one's body — breaks through into moral inquiry — he gets an erection. Our gestures grew fainter, whether human or material — my mother's face preserve within me the idea of myself — which took on proportion and power by the forces which came charging into her. After rubbing his hands he stopped by the community kitchen, passed the docks, wrapped in a woolen cape, knew equivo-cal joy, betrayal was already forming . . .

People start looking for their coats; voices murmuring, she stands looking around her. A bowl of flowers seems to be listening. Elabo-rate vanity puts a cigarette in his mouth. Never taking eyes from the match, mixing herself a drink, sits down in a chair near Johnny. She wrenches his eyes around that glass and drains it. Hard breathing — open the French doors — on his back smoking, a radio turned up loud in the next apartment . . .

He wanted to cut his message into the tablets of my mind, looked blank but knew my movements well. The night was clear in the reeds. It was thought, it wasn't a piece of wood. I saw a totally fabulous person appear over the top of the wall. I could tell from the closed eyes this creature had pierced the soft parts of his brain — searching for the circumstances of great shoulders — I might love a warrior, forged far away like that . . .

Or the time in school I saw an angel but couldn't get possession of what the sum was — the show, I mean — there wasn't a fraction of an instant — standing near the curb head thrown back, evaluating a smile. My stomach ran for the garage. Her face from the film was traveling in front of it. The spray seemed to catch fire. I fumbled along the lights, crying and laughing . . .

Outside the frost startled the frozen earth, a young boy happens to ask for particular stories. The same story you told before, by the washtub, at our first encounter, radiant with intrigue. The young men — one summer — the corn — birds with human voices — a gentleman with silver shoes — we had no money. The sky seemed large, public, embroidered with leaves; women crowded to the windows; the roof was covered with green moss . . .

He has her — the other in terror — but gave her no rest. He placed his hand as if they still were limbs and kissed the foamy waters. Make some happy burning bed at your side. How she said "no" to change her form while he sighed, the echo of a sigh made slumber deeper in those eyes. The seed swelled up, stretched both hands to heaven, columns the overarching skies, trembled to this high dwelling to see the world so far below me . . .

The tenacity, the ingenuity, shuttered each night, open together. The curly children flinging themselves beside themselves. The little chair — a connoisseur — remained in his grip. A goose to overcome the dragon, and mouth the flower of a clear ornate attention. At the zenith of its circulation visible in the face. Persimmons beside his place at table, a tingling sprig of mint between the sheets . . .

Be objects of contemplation, instruments of reflection. The original layout trails through demolitions, new building fever. Steamy atmosphere in oblique lines — between the pale yellow clouds in progress to Florencio de Abreu — were falling mango trees along the southwest outskirts — muddy torrents for the mud-walled pavilions — confronted each other a jumble of mammals established on these banks to carry a motor road. Functions were fulfilled so that these paradoxes might appear in public — arm raised in salute to suggest period grandeur, rose windows . . .

Did he receive the rampaging dogma allowed us? With lifted finger he pushes at the upper extremity. A woman sobs in silence against a pillar. I was falling asleep to the sound of the streets around his neck — it was indescribable, ecstatic in vibrating space — streaks revolved in front of my eyes, a man under a fig tree at a turning in the road. How you scream when my vigorous strokes have been opened to you! The skin stretched on the ground under their tunics. Blue veils bow down around a rose-strewn bed. Waving her naked elbows the constellations shiver. Coming and going — heart of the uproar — beating their hands in time — we lived in this street of the cutting edges, claimed by inscriptions, the superhuman beauty of a stone statue . . .

I watched their waltz — it seemed the invisibility became total — wedded by lovers' exchange to all the injunctions of uniform and veil. I was being mastered by a strapping body aware of his loneliness — fierce and pure — like a falcon inside my cobra neck. His solid thighs seemed heavier. Sailors trembled about the sun, secretly engaged. Observed by a tall blond — my glance was between his lips, spit in his mouth — the resewn pink scar fluid along the dangerous shores, waiting for me in darkest alley of the neighborhood. He led me the very odor of night. At the foot of the stairs these words which were too sweet, contained the sleep of a child against his body . . .

His face fills up with Johnny, oblivious to his surroundings. Rain outside, she snaps her fingers leaving the door open. Leather jacket at the window, he moves away, taps himself on the chest — the direction in which she pointed — one long swallow — a small hotel — passing a large framed photo of a girl with lazy eyes. He's flailing with his arms, comes up with thumb extended — her very shaky legs give way — asking you to use it — squeeze a couple of steps forward into the staring room. In a tall vase silence has trapped him — pushed around in a wet bungalow that rises to crescendo . . .

Opener of the roads, I was visiting in that map he drew on the ashes. It was a spot among intervals — sloping bottom between these chambers — except for the outstretched arms. Debris encompassed the city I'd conceived but left unuttered. I suppose our minds wouldn't come out of the pod. And the sound of wings passing over us — sucking noises torn out of the night — through the morass of this home which grew larger and larger, where a few false steps acquainted with secrets were close on their heels. My little baby striding toward me in moonlight — who was already high on his watery knees, praying aloud as usual . . .

She'd duck her head and look the other way. Her hair bent over my black and blue hand — receiving sympathy. Buffing her half-witted fingernails into the air and catching them in his mouth. Some bird which you and I wouldn't touch batted the breeze around — it's a disappearance, a gesture of good faith — into the rearview mirror where I left him, hands on his hips. I'd give her the exact address — it's someone else, it's another woman — in her made-over clothes pulling different ways — a creamery and a centerfuge — make me an offer — in a plain black dress that began to ache from her weight . . .

As in the saying, "Like father, like son," the houses weren't home. She devoured with red hair and green eyes the colored scraps of winter, afraid of her anger, was almost forgotten, reappeared in short skirts, freckled by beads and wolves' teeth. Warm nights woke the town — roasted sponge cakes and onion bread. Even the willow branches were decorated — young girls in a scissor dance — a bridesmaid scouring the sky for sunrise. She walked as though the powers of darkness were pious men and women. Her hair was a wilderness consecrated to me. Sitting up in a bed that resembled the heralding distance . . .

You see my face: a punishment, not a favor. Why put those plead-
ing arms around me? The driver doesn't know where to turn the
reigns — plunging animals — stunned and dazzled over infinite
acres. She saw the others and felt secure. No one can see us here,
this pool is holy. Her hands curved inwards, too dangerous for her
to plead with. The boy, seeking the game, had spread his nets upon
his mother — she stood still unmoving eyes — her shining star
being my wounds — he gave her back her human features, almost
on tip toe over the sand. And his passion blazed up to pull the cloak
from my shoulders — rising breasts — airborne — as though the
sight of shining men were driven deeper into the sky . . .

We're left undisturbed in the heated disorder appropriate to private
things. It's all decorated with multicolored trajectory like a hum-
mingbird. My correspondent quenched its thirst at good brandy —
an article of faith — I begged for a swallow — he shaped me pellets
of breadcrumbs moist with jasmine water. I can only interpret it
graphologically, arabesque, instructive. They bring me their strange
odor — hunting anecdotes that bristle with dangers — to put on a
spread for us: still-bubbling cream, featherbed, illustrated book. I
haven't given them away, I shall invoke sonority, a shape . . .

With a paraphrase indistinguishable from the local porcelain bowls.
A kind of latticework flour sieve made from split bamboos, trans-
forming, plaiting, creating a current of air to produce a collection of
specimens. You could examine the towns like a botanist examines
plants; one direction expressing order, the other, magic. I was
looking at men and women in airless cubicles — squatting in dim
light of single bulb — they showered sarcastic remarks on me — the
anthropologist — to underline their smiles — making a transposi-
tion to the manufacture of a laugh, devoid of mystery and unin-
spired by faith. We cross by plane to a single theme: the desert. The
tracery of crystals shade off into trampled grey — a continuous
surface threadbare by use — each shimmering impregnated, eggs of

the delta. The tone of a beggar lowering the voice on the last sylla-ble, as if he were saying "Why don't you do something to cancel out the element of cause and effect in the physical world?" Or squat down to urinate, nostalgically, in a state of equilibrium . . .

Dragging him along a dark stairway, the man whispers in his ear, bare of furniture. Light rays streaming on the walls, they talk about their families, standing in parallel lines with swaying bodies. That man was so beautiful it precipitated revenge. It passes slowly, as if a circle of great weight slipped from his hand. They surround him, console him, in the taut air on ropes. In the opposite cage, in continuous movement, he thinks he can feel their teeth. To have meetings with our brothers, our husbands, would take a door to the blood-stained bushes — blackened sponge — burying themselves in the multiplied soil — I once lived in that tree behind me — letting the world breathe out with both nostrils, in which I had shut my senses. The flowers of his face have become insensitive to light. I made a breeze in weakness — tell me where I can find Osiris — drank the panting river, green, vaporish, leaning on his right arm, overflowing . . .

He helped me, surrounded the secrecy of our first night. Beneath my fingers its heat — my whore — was born. His gestures powder him with a buttery softness — I leave a room on tip toe — excited by his blue trousers, laying my cheek against the keyhole in exile. One night he walked near me; I couldn't keep my hand from flapping his wing. I'm hurt by a physical ailment more secret than poverty, obedient to the nature of that particular polished steel, his fingernail. He was imagining himself in armor grease, penetrating his petrified shell. The loveliest infanta on his right arm, desiring abjection enough to be brilliant in his shadow. Laid out on a chair his jacket and shirt seemed inevitable. The procession started from the Ramblas de Las Flores at sunrise. I knew my place was one of them — their extravagant gestures — flowers down in a spangled skirt still remembered with stunning modesty. My shaken voice —

it hides a sharper, more dangerous element — smouldered within me, formulated a terrible glare in the middle of mantilla and fan. I'd never ceased to be silhouetted by the setting sun . . .

And if she was in a bar she just left disappointed, tears it up into little pieces too complicated for an ashtray. Glassy-eyed walks out to call it a day. Her head and shoulders on the wheel, staring straight before her. One of the bridges, spray of the tires, Johnny just looks at her. Strangers have friends like this. I guess I can learn to forget him. The highway lights didn't have any dinner, blindly past it. Steps are heard receding in a small coast town. The blinds are drawn, the radio is louder. She smiles in the direction of the chair in which Johnny sat, outstretched hand towards the telephone. Cars surf along the highway — people glassed in — wearing a scarf over her head, staring at her speechless glasses. I'm following a reason after the rain — cruise anywhere listening — the last passenger tight and determined and begin to get interested in restless conversation. "Who do you want to see first?" — he speaks without looking up — "and how long have you known him . . ."

We spent days at that place to allow the gases for such a digestion. The effects of his past debauchery could out-tire me. On our way I pointed to the edge of the pyre — two companions in a hole — cut to the irreducible minimum — in which case he might find himself by a process of devolution, missing. We were a curious procession that bordered the great artificial river, deep in the bowels of people who understood this swamp language. Again and again we lost the trail, separated from each other by high fragments — scattered a little body of men in that immensity — over trackless water, worn out away from home by the promise of pattern in the wilderness. I stared about me a flying light for a guide. It was as though a voice points to the east, whose temper in command here is discipline without law. Our state would have been different at its entrance. I'd mapped out his reasons; the reasons were curiosity. We were creeping towards the spot of enormous advantages . . .

Another showman put in a call to the city. Shaking hands and slapping backs down the street like he was selling tickets. I couldn't afford sentiment among the businessmen. He knocks down a big overgrown tomorrow to keep close watch on a dozen females. Across the street he looked out and saw me — made me feel like backward and forward was much too late — his mudhole eyes didn't have to move, lying around collecting dust. It started to rain a few happy drops: just part of the framework. Pieces chasing around a canvas during the ceremony to run things. When we passed along the side of the road their heads pulled up for the funeral. I sat down, stood up, shook the raining hell out of their hands. There was a rasping sound and the whole house rumbled. She folded my arms over the other — that's what made you cold — too late to change because we weren't the same people anymore — though you're all I have, you're mine now, splashing the windows . . .

Washing his hands the town was unrecognizable. The mud-splashed girls were grey and wrinkled. Monuments in the story brought their epilogues; it won't be held against him. A bride was led before his windows: she alone survived. It was summer air for charitable purposes. She started measuring the streets with silver combs, wearing shoes with pointy toes, filled bathtubs with lobsters to sprinkle the community with anything. Witnesses sat comfort-ably on a chair and sucked candy. From memorial candles the flames sputter — a moth wandering past midnight — you have to keep moving — the burden was mine to the reading table — of flesh and bones in the cleansing room — because a stranger can take the place of a person — size me up in their skins, vagabond — I tested her nostrils, red cheeks, pouring spine with arms outspread, trying to look in her face while my bed kept twisting and turning. If you're destined to live in circles her dresses were there . . .

Whoever you are with coaxing gestures that boulder will talk, tempted for information. It was a festival — grace of the procession

— outshining the other wheeling stars, smoothing his hair to wakefulness. Over the great muscles of grass bringing flowers, clinging to the wind. Those people coming behind kissed the unknown fields and mountains — made a low archway for the long head, writhing loops — wild with veins as he sprays another color, pressing under that weight — into a pool of the woods while she was bathing there. The only speech he has is not his own. Fear argues while he hesitates — cut through the mountains — both sides said nothing, secretly rejoicing — I must find the girl herself with reason, under cover of the yellow cloud. Full of the slang of rage he enters her mortal body; in that mating sewed up in his cradle — struck from each other struck them apart, embraced and ravished by the strangeness of his infatuation. Both sought his love; neither could touch him . . .

The little jewel and I have waited under the colored sphere. Of crumpled souvenirs what he alone held — ritual possessions — with tassels, without handles, a bunch of curls: the essentials. The sky turns the double curtain, enters my room. A little boy plays with difficult words so that she bursts her skin. A piece of paper compiled a list which demanded a burning refrain. We savored it, drank it, burnished it in the shadow — in the masterless house endowed with morning severity. Ripen the slice of cake under strawberry light, gormandizing — it wasn't difficult to believe in France in maturity. Our friendship attacks with gratitude her practical vantage point, striped with reverence. Unformulated the fragment that melted away — signs of a phenomenon — face to face, exhaled at the table. Fresh parsley with lemon made a gesture of withdrawal. She followed the colored trajectories, strewn around each breath. Blue paper, immaterial, with its great slow eyes . . .

But in the line on the hill he built a house the other day — up on the threshold, rub it between one's fingers. The name is recorded for distribution under the honorific title: Workbench — hammer on the black cloth — polishing it with a piece of glass — beyond the pine woods where the dusty sun danced in corners with distant gold — in his own house, Jerusalem, a dot in a book. Behind this layer another layer — books spilled on the floor — filtering in through cracks threads of golden bees, angels' sailboats. The overgrown pear tree completely white — silence with moss when no breeze blew — he trailed into late summer, door swinging. He kissed his mother a hissing kiss, and his father ran after him; he kissed his father's falling hand, ringing in his ears. Down the narrow corridor were sons and daughters — it was broad daylight — green flames from the silverware, red from the wine glasses — spinning around the table, miles away. He stretched out along the mound, a profusion of apple trees threw themselves down on the ground, blossoming and burning. He washed his hands, entered the house with reserve. In the whirling substance the floor remained — without looking up he opened one of the shutters — I'm here — and walked in the door. A half-filled glass was on the table. His small hands trembled as the food was served . . .

THE LAST HEAD I PAINTED

In comparison with different people, whose lives some people can draw conclusions from, my body is no immediate speculating attack. I came after an endless voyage after they approach the horizon. This excursion is full of what I've seen, which exactly gives that effect: the compact sky shows great hulks in the evening. One is overwhelmed by things — silent from the window — where you find huts and the living room — what tranquility — where I am now, that dark room, from an open door, collected; things adjust themselves.

Follow that little point between the green weeds and corn. I scratch memory: it has the same eyes they had. Without metaphor the same apple was or was not a thing.

Lamplight — which has light *in* it — will speak vaguely about the colors that have no name. Last week I saw a hesitation much greater than literal truth.

All that architecture, the sky, is calculated in one rush; in the corner individuals are walking. For instance *you* are walking, with pearl-grey eyes, in the open air, expressing what I want . . .

SOLILOQUY

His house on fine nights feasted on the contents of his kitchen — sight of a man leaning against the wall of his kitchen, and exclaimed, "The heart of the city!"

Young man, old man, sit down there when a window was flung open — full moon watering the flowerpots — my feelings (gentlemen) dismount and enter the house where the young girl lives.

She sat at my bedside. "Who is the youth?" "He is the son of my life." One for the pleasure of your company, and one for the robe of honor. Who changes others changes himself crowned with the proverb: "Your grandfather will forgive your father who is waiting to serve you."

I used to carry you on my shoulders — set before him a box of incense — and now I will carry this food to your house.

Holding my breath — he looked right and left — rushed through the door into the crowded street. Then, calling out as he ran, "I'm a man of the air eating and drinking with sleepless hands."

Take something from our common savings. I'll give him a mattress of silver brocade with an air of authority. He sat down on a cushion spread with silk.

Loveliness: the eyes of men. A tray of salt checked the flow of blood. He tied to his waist a bag filled with glass and gold. Putting on my best clothes it led me to this house.

THE NIGHT MIXING

She wandered from one scene to free herself — beige coat followed by tears — to another, and brought the clouds beneath the breeze — shadow of his hair — closed the window and read the date. Her grey eyes trace the mark, recite the brief letter for warmth, sinister under succulent crusts.

Out in the garden his twitching muscles didn't answer. Your little love nest of black hair trailing to his room — this freak thing in the long corridors — ornamented with electric lights as if cold air lengthened his steps. The crinkly blue light white as her nightgown . . .

This creature without a line — suavity into the hollow of the bed — took from marble hidden meaning, but didn't stop there. I have eyes shaped like fish, belly slopes like temple, hand drooped an over-heated rose, thinking bones, and the architect's naked instinct. I gather memory, silence, the easy manipulations of holidays, the threat of marriage. I had her gold malice, and his comradely snake. We're orphans (she clung to him) — the night mixing behind the windows, magnificent with shock — I rolled in a heap and began the jerky rhythms of correspondence, side to side like a doll.

All the sound of his voice acquiesced in the center of her being. In our home there's going to be an inundation — you and I ate the same well-trained dinner. When the clock strikes twelve: domestic optimism. I'm going to turn pale with adolescence. She was breathing. His eyes were wandering. They lowered over silent carpets. I draped an image on a background in the warm bed and cool room.

We lay waiting, side by side, united.

THE BRIDE OF FRANK

We were application — aerial shapes investigating their causes as
they unfolded their wandering life — possessed of temper, parents,
talent, fancy — in books in which characters redeem being from the
hands of infidels. I feel soaring pleasure.

When I was thirteen I opened my father — title page of my book —
to explain exploded powers warmed by a glance. To penetrate the
ocean behind the elements and give names — fidelity — from a
stream of fire reduced to electricity — over the malignity of an
alarming bed — the brightness of a familiar eye commences con-
nection: These are the faces cooped up in one place, and his sweet-
est voice hiding how the blood circulates, and my peculiar trembled
body, the seat of beauty.

At the end of two years every object inherited human feelings. I
paused and brain exemplified generation. His child pursuing these
reflections. My pale cheek with the tremendous secrets of fingers.

Winter, spring passed — watch the blossom— it breathed hard —
convulsive muscles of pearly whiteness — with his watery eyes
disturbed by the first kiss traversing my bedchamber. His eyes held
up the curtain of the bed. I remained listening, unfinished. My food
its white steeple drenched by the rain.

We ascended into my room, putting my hands before my eyes —
tingle — save me and save me — anticipated with such nervous joy
I became capable of shooting forth from the trees — it was a divine
spring — that night drawing me out I felt the sensations of others.

When shown the body they saw permission — I believe in inno-
cence notwithstanding temptation — whom you loved was a crea-
ture who'd fill the air with birds serving you — feelings worked up

by events — to wean us from our future prospects towards a tenderness of fainting limbs, a type of me. I was encompassed by a bodily cloud. I remained rushing at the window.

They congregated around me, the unstained pinnacle. I arrived at the same lulling sounds: the giver of oblivion. The ascent is solemn, curling in wreaths — I sat upon the glittering peaks — swelled with sunlight over your narrow beds. I beheld the figure of a man at some distance. As he approached a mist came over my eyes. You are community. Instinctively lying down I covered myself with little winged animals, light from my eyes. Spreading my cloak I covered the ground. One part was open.

It was a paradise filled with milk. Uttering a few sounds the young man had been filled up. I awoke into my voice by his means — sun on the red leaves — mounted high in the heavens using gesticulations and a gush of tears. Feelings of kindness and gentleness overcame me. Fringed by deep lashes, I contemplated my companion . . .

MEDIUM GREEN

I was going to be killed in order to avenge being touched. She tore into my blond mane — self-consuming — the vanities laid waste on the red carpet, split by the laughter inside me, this queen who whimpers and then commands my other name. I've practiced to conquer the past and everything which looked away.

Fear is the core of my curiosity. Spurting exhalations were too late — grabbed me out of other bodies — the witch jerked in my arms — I moved my lips in the posture of incantation, murdered at home.

Her crazed face will come true: scream of triumph! Who lived with him — how to live — exhibiting their weapons (feelings) drawn over my head and shoulders, the terrible beautiful one. Immortalize yourself in the present, fertility implicate me in this image. I slapped his penetrating face, his resemblance to the flattering expression of his eyes.

He kissed whatever he wanted but he seemed to want nothing. I woke up screaming to my mother and dissolved into signs — one evening at twilight — a meal prepared beside bed — who fixed the invisible boundary baring everyone's entrails, unapproachable, pierced, rolled up farther back to backtrack incompatible pictures, gorged behind an inconsolable chain of inclinations.

See: a child, a girl, myself, a man, an eyelash, a designated life. I know them. He knew them. Phrases coming out of your bed-chamber.

The makeup around the table can't help thinking of legends. I'd been kicked from the inside bearing a canopy to my eye. Aromatic gestures sell him something, suck him dry. Sitting at a table by a door who just came in with permanent roots.

That man is not irony but old curses. It, too, could still surprise us, made of human wishes. A monster hitherto unknown to me is in the oven.

CHANCES (I)

I rolled my fingers in my mouth, and brought his head towards me. I opened it and went in — library table — and sit down waiting in my private office. "Hello. I've been waiting."

He moved his lips — white smoke — in a certain rhythm, being a roulette wheel. Or you get in a box, bodyguarding, and a cool voice is calling you. I was thinking without hearing it, messing around a rhumba between his sleek hair and pile of shoulders.

He slid behind a purplish ironic smile — meat sound spread in the groove — and leaned at me: "Are you driving?" Squeezed out through big double doors — windblown distance of the damp house, driveway — and made the fog look small, a big man poised on the balls of his feet.

I swished a yard wide — soft bruise — dolled-up in daylight — his warm dirty hands that didn't match — pulling his curdled eyes away from mine to spear his mouth on a thumbnail. I leaned close and said, "It's a story in my fingers."

His name was — he was a — we went out — lead me away from the straggling houses and bigger moist concrete. At me softly through the phone, "Come through, boy. Come through." In pajamas and hot whiskey, head tilted back.

It's a place where two guys with masks between the living room never moved, having narrowed the blank stare to chisel a getaway out of it. It was about being excited as if they were home dragging a vacuum down the back of a pull-down bed — footmarks in the dust on it — that slept behind two pepper trees up the next slope. Jets of water fell out of sight like a stone.

He was scratching his hand with his beautiful teeth in his busy mouth. I don't like the way I got here but it was simpler on the nerves. Rub its stomach — there was a tableau in front of my face — I'm going out — I don't want to very much — inserted a hand sideways towards the door of the room — rubber ball — and braced.

There was no — and so on — coming after me.

CHANCES (II)

Back of my neck — the morgue — was pawing me over, I said, "That's why I'm not here."

He snapped his fingers. A body on frosted sheet sloped placid — darkness water — there was a hole for a moment, moved up and down with my lips.

Along the brown linoleum his arms down with the fingers of both hands pressed against his teeth — sit down — knock you off — thick legs planted his feet in the corner, a fairy tale. I stood up, looked at him, went past him, climbed up the dirty driver while his memory's fresh.

A few new splashes on his chin.

I'm a friend of his folded inside pocket bent over the spread. He growled at the face of the man in his mouth, bit hard.

As I went through, two guys popped, twisting so the sheered sun was a siren behind us. Along their flanks — into the scattered hills — down on the unused wild grass — a child in diapers, steep street in shadow, doors wide open like the spread ears of a kneeling man. The limp man snapped in the air, relaxed.

About that time I was lying downhill on his stomach. Sneaked a look — jerk off on well-spread feet — too many angles — drilled through his neck, his head, sagging: amiable expression. One said, "The guy was a hole," starting to shake.

It began to change color, darker than tired ecstacy. They come in and shut the windows to forget last night. All I had hid in the bushes with his thick fingers. Half-closed eyes go dumb on me.

CHANCES (III)

Glint of white teeth darted from the windshields of cars far below. He said, "Isn't the boy anybody done for a reason?"

"It was done to be framed."

The moon spat down the hill. It was late afternoon and I've changed clothes in the beautiful old house. Tall smooth house at my elbow — up a silk voice — I swallowed to feel terraces and a pale, velvety man. His spiritless cheek went past me — I began to lick his chest, businesslike motion.

I said, "We're all here but the two of us," and folded his hands against the back of his head. "I'll take charge of it now."

In his mouth he looked half asleep — huh? — a thug leaned over my chair. Both of us were shimmering; small, tight, a long way off. Darker trees jerked in the windows, smoke grey of the room. The room opens out of your neck — I moved the fingers of my right hand precisely.

Down hard on the floor — backed inward — his face in his hands. He stroked his eyebrows straightened out, polished the dough of his quivering chin — it was hard to stop shaking — I bit the end of his breath through a spray of smoke.

He moved his head about an inch inside the windows. I didn't think anybody would ever say anything again. I stood there licking my upper lip, got motion into my melancholy legs, and slid across the room. The room blows

up in your face, witnesses.

SMOKE SIGNALS

History — where they belonged (no documents) — collect seductive messiness in a glass-bottomed boat — could see a wine glass, could hear a knock on the door, and cried "Why didn't you tell me?"

"I'm your mother," she said. "I couldn't breathe until my hands painted these familiar things, smoke signals." A dishcloth on the vinyl chair tugged at her rubber gloves.

We talked about my destiny, the triangle of intimacy that makes her stomach so disturbing. Curtains were drawn over my neck. Physical is a difficult thing in a chalk circle. Coffee was having a meeting

in the kitchen — brown demon — end up in two pieces and burst a few geranium buds — polishing a great stone, a massive stone turret. The letters on the door read "Numbers correspond to browsers

and buyers." You end up here in this room. We can't see each other, stretched out sweating. She was the Queen blowing trumpet. All the letters contain weathered spirit, wise as they are.

"What will you do?" she asked, gasping at the shelf. It's necessary to distinguish the interior of things from the middle of the shell. At regular intervals I put my head under the pillow — my tambourine face —

fashion elementals — force field to control the outside breathing space of a flowing thing's huge wings. A dog, a knife, a raven, a mouse, a raspberry button, a river, a mixing pail, a shovel, turkey slices, a warm coat sleeve . . .

SLIM CEREMONY

The private sent the personal a present: stationary. On the top: "You know."

It was fall, for the weekend, for the smell of the air: distant; mouth open. Remoteness is a memory of other recollections. It had rained; under the trees sweat on dirt gurgling in the middle of night.

You drank water and felt a blister forming, the center of space. In a pose his shoulder associated with authority introduced me to exaltation. He told me to listen to the spaces in between — my breathing arrest — his clothes discussed the world — stripped to the waist harvesting my endurance. Lips, teeth, were the same challenge of vital statistics.

On the tenth floor the aria: "words bore no reference."

One Wednesday she remains within herself, not in words. Her slowness becomes a vaulting halo of despair. On the fourth floor they're flailing pink legs. Her full columnar neck older than the rest of us.

And in your mind — the reedy concealment — he needed to remember to believe how he was feeling — in the hotel in the morning — slim ceremony — we shook hands at the end of two weeks, squeezed oranges. Someone said, "Ambiguity was not a good winter for us."

In the spring it was safe to return, advocating violence. I wore blue shoes and blond hair. In the gym I felt a swelling that said "Please excuse me from physical education." The trees when you turned on the light were faces and nudes. I ate creamed spinach like real children.

As when one wakes spilling over the walls and complicity with power passes through your hand. Divested of acts themselves the picture must have floated in the water.

He walks out talking and the men are talking and he calls, "Hello!"

TELL ME

The show throwing out some easy rockets, followed by snowflakes. Then lilies, a titanic tenderness, tales of unadulterated symmetry, fits of baking cookies, especially in winter. Me by the window looking at the landscape — elderly relations — our street aware of the need to speak: *Tell me a story:*

> A little boy that shot up next door appeared to be made of a quivering voice and gauze curtains. His stiff-legged splashes brightened the streetlight trying to force us out of our homes. His forearms — two bedrooms — we arranged ourselves — submitted to pleasure under his ministrations — and kissed me roughly on the cheek. It revised my own pale lips.
>
> Beauty stood on the creaky hinge, huge and shapeless. My lush eyes grew bigger and bigger.
>
> A boy next door stiff-limbed sprouted a breeze. I breathed. This is your baby. Show it to other boys.
>
> I gently kneaded the world's grief. The house surrounded me with flesh. I was impelled. I disappeared. I did imitations.
>
> One night an occasional word would come into my room, my lips slightly parted . . .

Then that gesture imagined owning the exploded sky. Now he was a man like other things — restitch the fabric — polished stones — among the markers under the mossy roof, a thieving reverence. His face taking in evidence like a blade. Stuff its intentions into my mouth, I won't stand in the way. I am an apprehending moment: *Tell me a story:*

"IN A LITTLE STREAM OF ASCENDING AIR"

One mound with a tree — pages — basked in this red and violet spring. Big hats quivered after nights that sheltered the strawberries. An empty basket, "blurred and dewy", stirred by the greenery and children asleep. A circle hunting on its own.

A circle hunting on its own: Oak leaves may fill my mouth when my time comes. A zone more distant of signals — winds and light rays, a wall, a gate — because faith by jumping from wall to wall slid down her shoulders, and the walnut tree swallowed a vaporous leaf. She scanned the sky — levitation of the hydrangeas — *"It's all a question of the air they breathe."*

And letting my skin divergent keen among the rose bushes bear witness to another zodiac — loose but dormant — as the air touches it the subterranean chain — tapering fingers — will shoot light: juice and pulp.

There flickered in her face the month of July, repeating the ends of her sentences.
". . . rose to the ceiling",
". . . light there",
". . . covered the ripe cherries"

PELE'S SMILE

The pattern is local, with detailed information (free love) and that light upon the body from the nearest star: Immensity of Itself.

In the pantheon of months the boat sails under excessive heat — it sailed beyond him — summer of confidence and compromise — with one hand playing a melody over one hand that still dreamt of going there. The friendship between his gauzy brightness and the aureole of the sun blazed on (love was free) and the sails flapped on the horizon: Community of Spirit.

On Monday their moans could be heard drifting across the wind. I pluck the golden crown to make a toy boat — and gaze back at the receding shore. They laughed with the unfolding water: Maternity of Trust.

TO JOHN

In the scale of animated consequences, I put the seed into the ground — then *he* is one of the noblest perspectives — (but there were no footmarks on the wet lawn.)

Taken from this place within — manifestations of my approaching — pitched their tents in the valley, imaging the sky. You hung on the clouds, matured of that thirst to generate itself. Of his being a mirror would be held up to winding chambers — to be our presence there we could define perception. Braids in hand from you the winds pass (. . . *then I'll hide like a child in sleep* . . .)

I was walking in the city and turned the corner. The hill on which we stood was an assemblage of sexual motions in his eyes and lips. My companion, unembarassed, turned to his play. I'm an object of generosity for their residence with me. The instruments of a perfect republic on his pillow.

In walking he observed two men they came up to him. It falls into it, the waterfall of the stream. The pool is trembling in the light of noon. I undress — spray over all my body — leap from the rock — climbing into this fountain —

— and the curved lines opened by his smile transfuse from one language into another . . .

A man is beautiful comprehensively. I saw your ideal world on the footing of intimacy to contemplate its emanations . . .

TO JOHN

You bring *and* banish myself, so I'll send the rest in. The following things popped — expectations have been pushing each other — unpacked my books in the passage I found a head widens as it becomes bare — which spread, from a little hill, your whole continent.

If the nation is just beginning I'll walk east, west, north, south. He was there on the road for placing a man in the room where I slept. They breed these whistle leaves — gathers to me irregularities as opportunity — and looking upon ethereal things as materials of your swimming purpose, the trees when put in comparison have seen their dancing master. And furniture, onions, beans, cups and saucers empty on these events any pleasure of disposition looking down at satisfaction: *safety*.

He's neither here nor there but he came over to me and detained me. A wet night puts his hand to his head — speakers have passed — you were mounted on that face swelling into its intensity — scene-shifters away at an overture . . .

. . . at once the gradations and filling up whole . . .

64

TO JOHN

I had a mood of grateful organ, but everywhere.

True fusion barks in the night — at least he says so — he straightened up and turned to his neighbor: "There's no way to tell how serious it is," indicated the reclining animal, "but I'll see you this evening." Laid out on his back, feet in the air, his mind was on the day ahead.

At the heart of mutual presence entities had wandered to this spot. What they were doing: roamed, squatted, saturated. A great body was taking up residence, founding a new U.S. It oozed out in the living room from every object to supplant all things tangible — burst to his peculiar biological identity — within events in his living room, empathy ascending. A collage formed beneath his feet, and smelled the available sky — their thoughts — their individual attention — part of a hand there, joined to the metabolism inside him, another resident.

You, specifically, talk to me. He felt no surprise, perceiving an ancient departed chair. "Your name?" — leaving him to face the outside world by memory — "we'd have to make it up from the work" — he continued to leaf through himself, his tongue said "this one."

You come in — scents of sitting, or standing, or asleep — which healed as both eyes settled down to slumber — and he hesitated for a moment in a sidelong glance as the door slid back . . .

TO JOHN

Their song in a dress of feathers and magic bells — the singers stopped his introspection to listen, then leaned back taking his time with a ball-point pen. "I'll show you some pictures then ask you several questions."

False memories shuddered, took his place along the line of tracks. It takes experience to listen carefully.

I want what you'd do — I forget the question — it dropped to the floor he knelt down and groped — his hand if you reach in there would go all the way — I said OK, all right, while off to one side the body of someone and together inspected physical possession and ascended . . .

It's a list of human beings in social situations having to do with animals taking place in the spinal column and nervous system. You can test me out, I've been impregnated — his suffused face — they'd lifted into the sky spasmodically — I could handle your attention focused on that. He traced in the air — introspection and defense — the edge of a bed imprinted on his face.

Your measuring eye — ideology and representation — picked up the glass of wine.

Talk all you want. Talk all the way. I can tell by your face you were right . . .

TO JOHN

"My name," he said — spinning on the road — as though he were about to whistle — the city standing up in spears through silver puddles — "is nervous care, a rare thing."

The fabric of things in law sighed loudly.

Unmarked edge, shoes burning against a circle of red paint. You reached for the vibrated doorknob, warmth and light, put bags down again. He smelled wool, floral walls, a mirror inset with reading lights — throat in the doorway — when you want it, just ask someone, stroking the cool neck of solitude . . .

I have sharp eyes, unglazed wings. The name he earned stood out against the lacquered sky — wiped his hands on the thighs of his jeans — something rattled behind him, venting steam — like you were back here revealing old leaves — slit like a cat's eyes — with the sheen of apprehension dropping him off this balcony onto a higher personal building. And pursues his art where they'd left it, working on that arm of yours, his original conception.

It's your place. The man in a brand-new sleeping bag.

Find your way to the steady man's breath.

MAN OF THE HOUSE

Take back our front door, the washing machine, the dresser in the bathroom. Just a hazy world of destinations on maps . . .

He was standing in the kitchen as though on a street comer. Places I'd never been, worthy of another story — I closed my pulpy eyes — insinuation of the porch swing, settling down for the night — with your own couldn't-talk vocabularies born into you, to hold the unwilling light in my hands, humming the house . . .

There's his feet — I sat on my haunches and watched — pedaled up with a message to reroute history — he turned to me, kicked off his shoes — just for I believe tonight with secrets of his face lengthening until that-sadness-the-rain-dripping waves into the distance, people filling the streetcar. There's the neighborhood and inside the house. The hall up the steps. I back up and take a running start.

Then he's moving another breath, and when he moves my things are making their way from room to room. The way a person with one long finger can be tracing a vein.

It's quiet. "Where should we walk?"

It seems to glow in his pupils outside of myself, holding place.

LEGEND

M the heartbreaker had technique — plunder from her bedroom those confections of sustained body — and the angles selling her costumes — scarf around my head — die and drop petals. You could eat me up like this.

The walls — piece of paper — were lined with books, proving the ceiling was a rehearsal for the leading lady. She started erecting billboards bearing the phrase: "There was suddenly a silence . . ."

and loosened her rhythm, lost in familiarity, insinuate and toy the intimate, throw it away, scrawled with her lights a dignity driven to risk, that allowed a hint of improvement: every opportunity.

M gave her speech to the empty balcony. "I'm standing before a mirror to make a symmetry. Come along for moral support. I've slipped through the partially opened window — a great arc of postcards. It did look effortless because a gesture of reconciliation is taking place. Leaving was the closest I could come to forever."

RED GERANIUMS

She had an errand in town, put on her hat to reflect the clouds passing. At lunch, hooded with childlike exultation — plateful of green pleats — the allure of soup — she thought about subject and object, respect for wife and children, disliking dogs, and abruptly observed the wallpaper.

Her bird alight on the line like that — the living plank in the picture — quivering freak admiration — transferred the anguished rain of energy to equilibrium. She gave these exaggerations the burden of pure joy.

Tablets bearing inscriptions achieve intimacy; her tribute reduced a shadow to good faith. Grope children world power paint-box — an old woman with red cheeks drinking soup repeated the words "I'm the king."

IMPROMPTU

and I at night with a gentleness corporeal minced around in my
visible skin before the protective window like a damp rag against
the pink sky — spin away from their borders into blankets, flames,
the future spewing the past on my chest or ass. I jumped up and
paced the room — it was *mine* — collecting a thing of beauty
comparable to mountain peaks, the metaphor of my flying solitaire.
Excitation at four in the morning is a philosophy class.

I went out loving even my roommate, delirious with attention to
work, weavings, other people's ideas, drinking romantic coffee,
featuring me physically wedged in the sphere.

My life had material facts! (weightless!) and phantasmagoric
phrases (skull!). On a bus I even thought of my parents. The
droopy heads thrilled me about achievement and excellence. Every
chair had a heaviness from which sprang rationality and passion —
with my body proximity communal, cortex wave.

It was Sunday afternoon in a building arranging my clothes —
streaming necklace — surrender the flowers to the wind — the
intimacy of milk cartons — mutual corona — a concentrated
cigarette in an ashtray on the glass table

repose in anonymity the concrete landscape
"ravishment of the intellect by coming nearer to the fact"

LITTLE MADRIGAL

I know nothing. These are things in themselves — obscure plaster; evacuation matter — the night at his feet of which the reporter was to interrogate.

I saw him coming and my heart beat so fast the metamorphosis was on the tip of my pen. Little madrigal — leaped up and said: "The entire outer world listens, weighed down by personal interest. But hotly, and proofs exist." He opened his door to embellishments and revealed himself better.

But shame, punishment, mercy make us leap to the skies — I kiss your hands plotting out the acts and scenes — all the submissiveness such a great fall requires. It makes me shudder, this peril, so drink to my health. The trouble with correspondence is more details.

FADE

The heat got smaller, the sound of lapping water gathered around the car. I got out thin and shivering, arm around the pink towel. There are three parts: jumping, howling, and flailing. There would probably be a runaway scream.

The rhythm was full of pummeling oxygen; I did look down to my footsteps running. Berries border the trail; burnt sage rolled back to let me in. The bay beneath the slotted bridge — cream balls wearing veils, hissing and sweating in changing light. There are three demons: a hand between my legs, a mouth about to answer, a young surgeon in Boston. My body came to a stop.

I looked at the black liquid with its system of wires, living together in this black-crow wing next to the double plate glass. Floodlights would come by, blow a kiss, and say goodbye. I could still hear her singing, helping me out. My deadweight hands were red with kisses. One talker had cupped a hand over his mouth, whispered that a stranger was among them.

The sand whipped in the wind. I forced my eyes wide open, leaving a trail of red hairs. It had floated in a pattern, circles growing wider. I dragged my leg through the picture window. A woman was sitting in it, head thrown back. She turned toward me, with the round yellow spot in the middle.

I looked up, I pulled them toward me. A horizon from the city was riding the waves. With a gaze of permanent affection I open my mouth.

NO PLACE LIKE NOON

The eye shimmering liquid through the window — sky to the right — grazing on the vista point. Heat had softened his responsibilities — point of no return turning back — the sweat as its center of interest dangling from his curled lip.

He flung it into the empty room — dandelion seeds scattered at the city limits — for the days and the viscera in holding pens in the front. They'd squeal the clearest memories of children holding noses, dripping what secrets such a drainage could hold. Holes elude capture.

He walked up and down the length of each house. He couldn't tell which was his to choose — thick shaded corner — I'm looking for a nervous laugh that lived behind her screen door — that big torn evidence — to read the name on the mailbox where he stood.

The burning faster neighborhood gathered the bloated shells swinging from garages — his wooden mother, little brother taking a nap — located intact in a peanut butter sandwich, still there.

He sat in a swing set and shook the beating sun off. The heated air was a magician:

There's nothing here.

SUBLIMINAL SWEAT

The sky like my body was a sprawl of expatriates. Some nights — spare parts — he seemed to belong to two men and a woman. The surface tension — subliminal sweat — touched sparks from the mouth singled out for him. Sleeping face fragment previous century narrowing the meat with a hole rolled straight into historical desire — staring through a window. They were mounted against their centers under which he voyaged, spelled out in a constellation of pink mirrors and bulbous clocks . . .

The sky like a cobra was swollen in his jeans; his next step might make him feel better. Fridays, Saturdays were still there — and the specialists drifting through the crowd — him with his usual hypnotic calm under the droopy lids, fuck-bulge mingling with adrenaline some very approximate way. You could throw yourself into a field of data, scattering sailors in the pit of his stomach, a hologram hormonal in a black t-shirt, splashed at the far end by the stood-up cobra in full extension . . .

The sky like an alarm on the edge of anxiety was hammering for the window, conscious of what he'd done, been done to. Face forward in a square of faint light — transparent shaft — it passed through his fingers as some combination of wind and dry ice, molded in languages extending his pink manipulator. Heaped muscle on the table top. And drew a line above her cheekbones tipped with burgundy — collecting you from sliding glass panels — invented to speak again the components of freeze-frames . . .

The sky refilled his cup like when you're not looking. In the dark down his spine flickering figures — he lay on his stomach — straddled him again, fragments of arriving and receding. On the coffee table, in the desk, it had been cut away by literal hands — nothing personal — as a temporary net screening history of ticket stubs and rugby shorts and octagon plugs and a new French passport. Cigarette smoke reproducing the movements of men ran after him. A boy nimbus lit from behind was erased in a rainbow cloud. Afterimage of cooked meat in the glare of a flaring match . . .

The sky in this town like a hard mouth was pressed into a thin line. He went cartwheeling around the street — business connections — with white hospital chairs blinking in the doorways, as private as the rest of our shopping list dissolving inside you. A continuous flood of city lights shook his head. His country burning beyond the subject — "it looks like" — extracted featureless from the envelope, the tiara itself patched into his forehead. Tell your partner that he willed himself into passivity. Tell her the crowded street compensated automatically . . .

Like memory lane the sky was a collage of dark eyes; pretending to be a predator it probed for gaps and mapped the route he'd take. And sometimes flooding back she wore white pants and felt like laughing — shuffled the deck — tell my people I'm holding the crumpled bodies — spilling out of elevators, street doors, lobby, swirling to the one who spoke: "I'm on my way." The wall behind his back mirrored the message — matte shadow of his arms in a dance, peeling back the refuse that had grown at the white table on a scrap of paper. It was a beautiful arrangement

like a Paris sky, compiled on the open market of generations. He kept those hind legs moving. Someone reading over his shoulder found paradise. Scrawls of light mold against him — assembled a wrecked voice in screaming jags of moonlight — sing, virus — through the sweat-damp sheet dripping to testify. And diagnosed on the outskirts of an experimental program, playing ghost when we got there, he polished the confused memories of childhood and watched the sun rise. He went to the window. It was raining sluggish sheets of clear plastic as it disgorged conversation on the phone in his hand . . .

The sky leaned forward, speaking in a navigational tone, began to stroke him gently. "Okay," he said, "I hear you;" the foam ran through his dark hair. Past a newsstand, a bank, a tourist place, a sexual cubicle club, across the fabric and tendon — vibrating buzz — expanding sheets of light while the live things arranged themselves against the pink morning. He leaned forward on an animated sea of speech that never left him — Personality inventory; Public invasion; Jurisdiction flexibility — feeling his own lips move into position . . .

Blown away by the blue eyes in orbit through the floating maze of paper faces — the glassed-in gift shop — he plucked at the ragged audio hood, single organisms coded with corporate identity. A posture of invisible lines stripped back to ancient history, steering that thing upstairs. He'd seen the men affect the semblance of men. He crumpled the paper in the pocket of his jacket — heraldic smile, bird in flight — out in the warm rain drifting across the sky as sky. He intended to use this place as his home. The face rotated. He could smell his own sweat . . .

HIGH HEELS

Who wandered through her apartment, got ideas, had one, held her mouth fiercely drawing out their heads and guided them down the hall to take off their clothes. If it was a young man: lay down in the private painless thing. The boy's heart abdicating responsibility — she entered advocating strength and power — to stalk the center of his clear voice full of attention. She swallowed. "I've been looking forward to meeting someone interested."

When you got used to her her tight lips — a tailored grey suit — prolonged time, flickered mid-flight — she tilted forward, sitting and blabbing, reconstructing the men to satisfy erotic cravings, the evil planet of right-hand people. She unfolded her legs. Cruel people regarded each other as she caressed the same species, patting his bulk — he kept saying, "I'm sorry" — dizzy with intimacy, the graceful complexities of personal contact. Shapes of young men in shorts were lining up. The underdog of great accomplishment — helpless fuck — stood defiant, glamorous, overwhelmed with how small he is. Head down, her nervous throat whirred. "I'm busy tomorrow."

Safety had dried out. The tremors of that inquisitive stiff crawled along the floor, fluff of one blond boy shadows. Sun caught the window and floated in midair. Her idea of nature to get cream for her melancholy strength, illustrated by a pink frog — she constructed holding hands — his personality on a leash, against a ramming soundtrack. The room filled with events, carrying her ponytail. She stretched her legs regally. "I'm tougher."

Who screamed in a ceremonial kitchen, fascinated by the boy in darkness. He started glowing. She put her arm around him, sucking his thumb. A person as a healer as though my legs were infinite. "I metabolize objects."

When her fear about childhood spanned the floor before her they were there, upright, solemn. She squatted, surrounded by mini-skirts and a rhinestone tiara — his pant leg shaped to look like a bridge of concrete, its sleekness ennobled by efficiency and order. She stripped to the waist before the mirror and licked the fog off. She climbed on his uncomprehended lap and said, "I taught you something."

These broadcasts ripped up the trees, the singing home, the hall in twilight, the nuclear school, the bus, bus-stop, transistor drugstore, the grocery, the battered kitchen walls. They pounded out names in the rain big enough to fight back. It was voluptuous or wounded. It was gulps down the street whipping her legs — a snowstorm went to hell seeking relief — the hound violation — in which she would lie in bed, irrelevant, evoking the dazzling pink threshold yelling "We're here!"

People have yards in summer, cookies, teased hair. She moved back and forth around his glandular neck, breasts massaging. Then the slapped face — ornamental flourish — raw, hot, deferential. Her stretch pants — target on the fence — showed each condom leg — the sudden stiffness of his troubled receptivity — induced her ferocity. Genitals stood on the rooftops and cheered. "That'll teach them to be decent."

In a position of slumped passivity humanity was fascinating — the stranger's frozen face with wet underpants — she flung the raw curtain back — his blank transient eyes observed her size. She heard him say those things — listening for it — smiling, hugging, loose-limbed — reeking with the alien music of a soft voice. The whole composition of a dozen or so boys was brooding to reverse the tide. She was enlarged by exploding gentleness and big hair. "I'm roaring."

Who, laughing in the bedroom with the door open, pulled his face across her lap with majesty and squealed over and over, "It's fun!" With trembling fingers she acknowledged pity. The clarity of inflamed boundaries lit the night. "I saw my formidable opponents and turned our faces to beauty and pleasure." She was profoundly satisfied.

ONE MORE STEP

He never lied but talked incessantly. In the crowd nice things were talking, returning for encores. He was floating watery between a spongy mess and his father. Beyond the boulders in the distance the landscape slept home.

The whole place ran at the sink as he emerged waving at the neighbors — eyes shrieked with laughter — when between his teeth the horizon proved difficult. A few feet to the left (he didn't dare move) (he cocked his head) time and place sitting there like that no longer felt attractive. All the weight was beautiful in the dark.

Feet first in another clearing he sat looking at the sky. He reached out to push through it from above.

It was so soft, obliterating the home furnishings. The viewer vaulted up the stairs, standing there with the door open.

His fingers were going to take care of themselves, talk to each other. His intestines couldn't think where he was, then bloom out of the ground. He stopped and looked down — took hold of an arm — into the silent box in the morning light and thinning air. Consequently, the shrinking sound around his head hissed.

What he was doing about the glorious secret gave a special warmth but no proof of permanence. They seemed to vibrate and engulfed him. He walked into the house he was into the center of the room.

A large planet had given way, bent at the knee. Pulling up his gown he felt oxygen welling up inside — adoring crowds — by kissing that foolishness as the room rocked — diving headfirst at a hill in the distance that appeared to be holding its stomach. He pointed at the window and waved back. Shimmering muscles light.

HUMAN IMMUNE

I lie in your arms. I kiss your mouth. Use your nails, creature. Our roles — the crown, the infractions — inhabit this sanctified place to the point of fanaticism. I have to get my hands on the world.

Dead from complicity in San Francisco discharged me, the harp of a person had an arc. Then listen to inhale the contagion, where in the trap of your consciousness you have to pull to get out. Himself alone and scared kill mercies. The body has powers to paint yourself purple.

And shifting grasses, such erosion and mosses, nightjars lived on the droppings of sunny days . . . in that country of circumstances and moods — shattering its bark and throwing pieces of it around. Facing away from the entrance, with jerky movements kicking the sands backwards. I saw the size of a hand, losing hold of it . . .

Birdmen, across the rising hills and bay, rolling naked one night stirred and rose to the spell. He's out there, into the dead stumbling mind. I'll be accounting for no memory, without so much as a template. His nostril is hissing; his tongue in spasms. He has several parts on a breeze, an asylum this story surrounded. The face ripping wide open has led a team of men in white gowns and slow rhythm.

And twinges we ourselves devise woundingly by miscalculation — delicious conflagration winking — to become familiar and to pulverize them all. Curves could hope to find in this world no more beautiful hair. *Hell is round.* I squirted them with kisses. On his back at the edge of the couch to die of pleasure, kneeling into your asshole to form around me. Comprise our friends the memory of the moments they passed in that virtue. Their honor therein, helpless before desire . . .

Where are you now, the harder you pull to get out? Then is that person fixing little sandwiches and watching TV? The Bay was fucked — ornate theories — there's the previous photo of "husband", hippies, Pt. Reyes beach, leering face, pink light, someone else. A portion of scripture, undiagnosed. The placement of objects is a language theme, no longer private. A little old hairless man had swollen up. Pain is healing me into submission, he wrote in his journal the secret of the universe: *hell is round.* You flop and thrash in fact.

The homecoming was marked and mapped; they circled in ever widening loops. Processions migrating on blue nectar — stopping in the rising air over coastal waters. I waited I repeated I waited the test. The results were not fooled. I spent the summer as a natural landmark — the bearer of delicate organs — leaving the destiny dormant on dry days — moving my wooden ship to research, under spell of the spray. The sun was gigantic, slow, low-hanging. We had to acquire some knowledge in this year, food for a narrative. Summer is short. Inquiry raising our eyebrows was contagious. Moonlight on meat.

He knelt down next to me — fallen giant, empty stump. Feeling the blood pulling around my thighs, "I think it's screaming," I said. He stood barefoot, one warm leg, nest at the belt, pink wriggling sack, I wanted to run into the sun now, bristling muscular bulging animal sedated by his eyes. My body shook against him on a hot summer day, gushing to life, blood-filled, blood-dizzy. He rolled over onto his side, watching the men. A ruin. A patient. Overgrown so that the flat air had no answer. We floated in which the memory moving our bellies going dark have all taken flight — a cure may be possible — tell me what words mean — pleasure for a coffin: turn and enter your home.

The ghost which leads to burning incense on the altars of magical friends — these gods come upon gods which erects them — confections of the deific — showers down events, the smooth operations of insignificant romances to penetrate into their historian's hearts and foist upon the reader authenticity of the marvels . . . At last he dies, this exceptional man who loves them, phantom spawn, fraudulent cures, boundless poverty and the images of objects. Just a while ago I gave you attentions pure and simple. I take the oath worthy of your friendship exterminated in me. The lancing pain stuffing me with bucks and thwacks to distill soul's fuck: slip away, leave the rest to me, initiated into our mysteries . . .

With the Sixties the Seventies in Berkeley shot forward for replay to put the spaces where he wants — stars in the universe suggest metaphysical poets — lingered in remission studying the cosmic characteristics of T-cells. Triumphant skull in the grin of his malady, whacked as he was in a feedback loop. It's necessary to interpret men compared to sleepers in a private world. Two men pass through a forest which passed for the real world. From the cardiac ward through the underground corridor to encounter arrhythmia on the cathode screen. His head, his heart, a wave-form. And he spoke his monologue directed outward from the wisdom of a body: *hell is round,* the little clay pot locked up. The dream-time of heroes trying to throw-up names: California, Parsifal, Chuck . . .

Night fell and a moon showed up between peaks. We were given a welcome for centuries. Aroused by smell in their human behavior a growl in heat, with a mixture of affection and respect. A little whipping, a little touching it lightly. One sometimes hears the ice snap with a seam in the center; large numbers breeding in our district at those breathing holes. Members kill themselves, interested only in sugar. Suddenly the door was flung open, a youth tumbled in; the event we'd been preparing for changed our life entirely. To wake up to stop the alarm clock with one hand I lay on my right side facing my other — my Other Side — pressing the human places in a firm grip that woke us up in horizontal posture turned to face each other, covered with a thick blanket, the murmur of description, connected by an invisible rod as resistance fluttered back and forth.

The end of perspective, the proper shapes, blobs and pillars and singing minarets. You're a mess in the park. You're a willing dirty dog. With the sun disappearing a low fog tucked-up the air. I slept resting on the windowsill, stranger than birds. I used to be little but when we came back they were gone. Overnight to hear whatever was to be heard. With its overgrown boxed body jerking in perfect symmetry, this wizard — see what there is to see — bruised in deep breaths, and an archaeologist invited down to watch. He'd like to go from the bay to the ancient golden hills into the earth unannounced and never saying where. It was like some mechanical body secretly unstrung leaving accretions of soft dirt and mud. He kissed his waiting hand with both hands. The warm competence of the finished parts as if such machines had meaning. Touching it, the thin shell, tucked-in facing the bay may lie quiet in the dusk.

A way is opened; my initiated companions go after. Each gave his confrere the pleasure of sensations, sprawled on the stone floor. Sucking a moment of suspense into calm to savor its entirety, the combination of prick and ass and mouth, an eternity in that delirium he'll lie in your arms. Common measure in homage to fitting company. We'll make a circle *(hell is round)*, I want that energy while speaking, place yourselves close by me, excessive behavior swell discourse in proportion, the carnal prosperity of an everyday affair. It ripens and is born, having provided circumstances. Made an incision running around the head, then removed the strip of skin. Your body, the altar, on the altar. Go consult the children of love. There are minds, my friends, certain spirits, having rid themselves of vibrations, having progressed from extravagance to the speeding star, plagued in whose name passion alone dared multiply. Come — this'll serve as a bed — fuck my ass into my mouth.

This is what the dream referred to as *hell is round*. When he got out of the hospital it had the effect of wiping out history. Right now, the city was in intensive care, locked-out behind him. In the small room huge eyes flaming. His fried mind projecting on each side a sword to conquer — through the sense organs through the rain through the ward through the trembled fields of flowers as if shape had no substance through the living information completing itself. The blood of communion turning is a strange sentence. It broke through and fired experience at his head. Penetrated man penetrated himself. He was dragged through his address book deconstructed as official documents — the only way open. A limbo in lymphoma contemplated itself: he lived it, he loved himself, would love that too. He saw it spread out among us, pulled from his body. He could hardly wait to abolish himself, freeing him to go commando saving people, glommed onto another pretext in grief and love through the magical powers that underlay all his saved-up strategy . . .

I have variations about what was there: fathers, sons, and grandsons. When the sky cleared the weather superimposed corrections, noticing and recording more details. Fly to an elevated lookout post. It's my intention to describe history at the place we left them. Populations of flesh caught in our net. Of their courtship, of their species: their back was connected to display-movements fading toward the warm neck, a pirouette. Small circles this ceremony for hours on end. About the organization of behavior: some of them visited me. Animal behavior in the summer of 1956, or '76 — embarrassing luxury — while we were floating on the shore or in the sea or under veils in quiet corners as the haze hanging behind us . . . Feverish outburst played havoc with their exact pose while sitting indoors, digging out of the morning for tests, returned positive results on the same day; distance . . . I've made a number of flights already — round flat discs — homing. Then my legs stopped moving altogether. Under the full microscope ferocity with nerve endings waiting I hovered, motionless, maneuvered into position.

I will see him standing, pounded, irresistible. In the dunes of my thick woolen sweater, dropped off along the western edge, panting through the indistinct sand, puncturing the middle of the farthest horizon, arms raised. Through the muscles of aching arms and legs opening on my back to the sea, wrapped in tangled sunlight staring beyond him. What I didn't think or say fill my mouth, the terrible mysteries of sleep and navigation. We're best friends ever since ever. I noticed you in class — my full attention — if given the opportunity stammering to encompass love stanzas. Have you smiled? — choreography! Are you wrapped around my waist? — cosmic winds. San Francisco the beauty can take a picture — the air around him. I lay there on the floor, dug into the trenches, throwing down his trousers, the root of bones and mud and blood. I suppose he once lived here, curled into the tails of my nightshirt. He walked past me in his undershorts, an organism We are the owner of sight and speech. In the grey light west of the Great Highway: not even me. We sat in silence, a blanket covering his lap. If you flew by you'd see these imposters, vapors of tenderness. It could never be contained.

AMERICAN THINGS

A housewife lost the baby, a muscle looking back. Late at night, her slurred stomach was listening for a heartbeat.

The letters she might write, the finger with the ring, her birthday endlessly fade. Those big American things through the rear window through the emptying sky. The grass reached back and imagined all the water in the mud — stick figures taped to the posts. These objects to the attic: weightless pictures in a wasted lap.

That's where, round and round in his old recliner, spoonfuls of whiskey, he's thinking of her, scattered feathers. I looked up at the windows, sniffing boxes, perched on a ladder rippling with waves so that my eye hurt — slam of aluminum screen door — while I chewed and swallowed the room and walls because nothing about him had solemnity or anything where anyone might happen, possible motion.

"We're going walking" — as though at some point my aimless torso had an extra dimension of space. I pinpointed, in the distance, what he wanted me to be, what we wanted him to be. The vacant house had left stretchmarks on the horizon, a little rectangular white in half-light. It was the pallor of an exhalation, raised by synchronous breathing. Without a body in repose, without the image of a young man, without her veined shoulder, without a yellow cupboard, without without-knocking or sat down next to me on the platitude bed or picking at my food or submerged hands in dishwater, without submerged hands . . .

JINNEE

One day which stood numerous — a great wooden trough — passengers paddled with my eyes until resigned to myself closed in.

One day in the distance as I drew nearer a man emerged from the ground each month and questioned me: "What's the restitution, and when will you come hide in our hiding places?"

One day my absence dissolving climbed into a tall tree: a cow, a buffalo, an elephant, elephant fat, apes, locusts, a black fur, camel lips, tore the body to pieces with his fingernails, a dog asleep snoring which filled our hearts with description, a donkey which resembled a cow and a sea-bird.

Seeing the violent world — eminent merchants — one day naked men with a strange ointment anointed their bodies. Their distended bellies reaching the rolling plains — go on across the grass to the opposite side. The markets and well-stocked shops gathered around to bid me farewell — I lay in a corner with a leg bone so that the ornamental air would come back with terror, and I was rapturously welcomed.

One well-trained day dragged out the young bird. The sun weighed anchor in the ominous twilight, crouching upon my shoulders, one foot against my belly, kicking me every time I stopped. After weeks of servitude I began to ferment, tripping around the trees so woozily I'm known among the travellers as 'Washed Ashore'. I ran to the edge of the tilting deck and said, "I'm a very old man. I have been young and beautiful and the men grew wings on their shoulders and for

one day flew in the air — all his possessions my possessions — to allow me to cling to him took hold of his waist carried me up swiftly into the high higher . . . I saw two faces coming up towards me. 'Who are you?' 'We are your worshipers.' 'Is this how friends behave?' 'We are the bonds of friendship.'" Leading him away the boys kissed him again and again with tears running down his cheeks. "Mother," he cried, "that man is my other mother." It would be a grief or a wealth in his need. *I am here, master — I am here at your service!*

THE WANDERER'S NECKLACE

So they sat down and drew the curtains; part in that feast in my marriage bed is given at funerals, after which her beauty has the power to bitterly repent . . .

Or of a time, traveler, motion represents a minute's pause about to speak to me. He took that individual's hand and put out his forefinger — the little machine jumped — the psychologist looked under the table — traveling through a second impression through the space in which it had already been.

One's going into the bushes on probation, conducting tours for sunstrokes into the jungle dressed up in pink and gold like a Nazi marching song. There's so many of them now that my pelvis is a musical prodigy. She's traveling with the military escort who organizes morale-boosting vomiting — recital over gorges and chasms — through icewater rain through an earsplitting rendition of "The Texas songbird opens her mouth and out flies flies."

And if I hadn't written "salt" or "mustard" there was still talk about victorious white powder and extemporaneous forays into German words meaning "remote distance in space and time" and "a few ventilation hoods qualified for physical survival." What do you think of the Jew who never reached this point of tenacious insolence — a shepherd of mimetic plants, a shaman of rock-climbing cows — climbing the rocks with things one can see and touch but studying centuries of trial and error to remain faithful to matter? They made nails on iron plates on charcoal forges pointing skyward. Where strawberries grew up rock walls in the cracks of cow dung halfway up the side facing the sun in a few dense syllables that permit you
the luxury of
they rang like bells.

That a woman doesn't wish for vengeance had been prayed for. That they were blameless, blinded, misled, summoned, chosen, chanced, forgotten, unnumbered had been creeping forward until her raised prow — the unreadiness of our ships! —dragged from the sea the sound of groans and he who was watching strove to kill himself. I inherited the cause that had been noise abroad. The head writhed in that strange loneliness by which a mighty deed is moonrise — with your dreaming eyes when we rode together to Ragmar, to Iduna, to Elsewhere lost in the battle of the ships — gazing at us both in the burnished glare of a story almost lost to me. One was a necklace of puckered pearls that burst out laughing; one was who I think I am in my own language.

The lamp in his hand, his head in silhouette, his blood-stained socks. A faint glimpse of circling stars gaining velocity. Purple bushes under hailstones, tall spikes of white flowers, shredded. I examined them as I squeaked through, and it struck me that past generations were heaps of fruit, flinging peel and stalks with their hands into geometrical patterns, faster and faster from weeds and fungi: flowers, and the process of putrefaction was a social triumph, all that fierce commerce and traffic connubial against eternity. A little rubbing of the limbs soon brought her around; she slept in droves in a tumult of apprehension. Colorless; ape-like figures running up the hill carrying her dark body.

Last night, seduced by a man, I have a little shadow — what size shoe do you wear? — a complete capitulation mopping his face in the position of a hammock — I want another beer — when I started night-fishing, hold still, that's the mystery of him . . . Last night in his socks and shoes, stuck in the itinerary — but innocent has been my *specialty* — I passed out bottles to give it a personal thing — put your hand on my arm — the buttonhole so frayed his chest heaves while you bathe in sweat, the black banner of your poet's hair . . . Which way is the murmur of the sea? He lifts a branch of wild orchids to help them draw bees in the sun. In twenty-five years of travel this is the first time we've arrived in a perambulator, teething on longevity and a couple of salt tablets. Oh what is attention that has turned inward among the tables as if all the poems were written a long time ago, roused in the light of afternoon bathers heard from the beach? Generosity passes through the Sierras: it may rain before nightfall.

We were taking place behind a curtain, not perceived but not forgotten. Blessed be he who exterminated my questions. There were rows of cupboards packed with obsolete fauna, molecules in a liquid state, chlorophenol, benzene, Ibsen, and Thomas Mann. He didn't hesitate to harpoon the regulating universe in the presence of sodium, to rectify the inexhaustible basement in an aluminum pot. Significance is neither rigid nor elastic, but floats like ampules of a holy relic. All patchwork differences lead to consequences on an illuminated parchment kept in a drawer. Through Poland and France the mustached messenger opens his mouth, an appointment at the railroad station, an artificial crater. Encircling tiers constructed of steel, the oscillation of a corolla to figure out the final purpose of the open valve — as she watered the flowerbed — something did emerge from the game of anonymity — and took walks around the brim as if the distant howls of dogs really nested there, about to spring.

"I am a captain, what are you?"
"I am an other woman."
"Why do you wear that necklace?"
"I am the woman who wears it."
"There was once an emerald beetle I saluted. Why do you spread your glittering dress before me?"
"You are a fool."
"Will you be my friend?" She answered: "I couldn't mistake your retreating presence for the odor of forgiven."

I sat peering down that well. I sat upon the edge of the well where the daylight race was so plausible and ornamental industry has its birthright in the sky. I burned a match to banish these signs, pallid bodies of worms in zoological museums. I said to myself, "You are another match, striking open space." I heard the breathing of a crowd of beings being gently disengaged. Those pink lidless eyes made me giddy while they stayed peering and blinking up at me and I staggered into the sunlight kissing hands and ears, kissing paws and old habit foot, arms dexterous and the tall pinnacles of shoulders, with an air of expectation that they'd receive my tangle of branches thick with dust . . .

And sewed up in canvas — gives me the shivers — I saw him going down to the beach. You struck me in the face and you twisted my arm and you rushed into my cubicle and we rushed out to catch the sunset — adjusting the flowing silk about to fold on the road — hypnotizing the orange trees wearing clothes of the opposite sexes. Let's kneel down together in the kneeling position conducting services in praise of . . . in praise of; let's excuse the thunderstorm that broke your windows and doors, materially speaking. The odor of his sweating forehead is birds scream in the rainforest, a restraining gesture of an almost voluptuous kind. Off, off!

My country is different from this one — I mean my language — I'm not my father, I'm not black lead, I'm not veins of glowing metal below the ground. My country to do it and lost by it but not I; left when still young, walked along the stream eyes to the ground, saw a stone picked it up, prospector, precisely to find out whether the rock is finished; I'm not finished. My event doesn't talk with anyone about the subject. Even the last hour of the day must be dedicated to dismantling the day.

The tongue had been slit, consolation, that she believed this world to be weight in them — hiding places, for what were the high surrounding walls? — that the split tongues could deal out beneath the tree starlings — that she believed this to be world weight in starlings. She spoke the words sobbing as though a hand couldn't see where it was guiding. For it was these words that should have lived, should have been spoken, should have mattered.

And great sheets of green rainwater the thing itself worn away. Of objects in some covering sloping with extreme slowness.

To be quiet for a while I'll try to imagine your now almost phosphorescent skin.

Designed by
Samuel Retsov

Text: 1o pt Plantin
Titles: 13 pt Plantin Titling

acid-free paper

Printed by
McNaughton & Gunn